HP Sauce
My Ancestors' Legacy

HP Sauce
My Ancestors' Legacy

Celebrating the coronation at "The Sauce"—1952

Nigel Britton

authorHOUSE®

AuthorHouse™ UK Ltd.
1663 Liberty Drive
Bloomington, IN 47403 USA
www.authorhouse.co.uk
Phone: 0800.197.4150

© 2013 by Nigel Britton. All rights reserved.

No part of this book may be reproduced, stored in a retrieval system, or transmitted by any means without the written permission of the author.

Published by AuthorHouse   06/24/2013

ISBN: 978-1-4817-9703-0 (sc)
ISBN: 978-1-4817-9702-3 (hc)
ISBN: 978-1-4817-9704-7 (e)

Any people depicted in stock imagery provided by Thinkstock are models, and such images are being used for illustrative purposes only.
Certain stock imagery © Thinkstock.

Because of the dynamic nature of the Internet, any web addresses or links contained in this book may have changed since publication and may no longer be valid. The views expressed in this work are solely those of the author and do not necessarily reflect the views of the publisher, and the publisher hereby disclaims any responsibility for them.

The HP Sauce trademarks and copyrighted materials used in this book are owned exclusively by Berkshire Hathaway, 3G, H. J. Heinz Company and its affiliates and are used with permission.

Every effort has been made to source potential owners of any images not acknowledged.
The author will be pleased to do so in future editions if contacted.

Contents

(1) "Britton" and "Britain": Who do you think you are?......1

(2) Vinegar and Spice 41

(3) Uncle Edward and the Eastwoods 55

(4) The Midland Vinegar Company......................................101

(5) Visitors to Aston Cross..115

(6) Harry Palmer's HP Sauce?..121

(7) Harold Pink's HP Sauce? 127

(8) Houses of Parliament and HP Sauce?............................131

(9) Garton's HP Sauce?..143

(10) Mary Moore's HP Sauce?..157

(11) "Saucy Business" 161

(12) Samson Moore's HP Sauce 181

(13) The Midland Vinegar Company Limited......................197

(14) HP Sauce Limited 207

(15) Aston Cross to Elst, Holland..233

(16) Illustrations and Photographs 243

(17) Chronology...249

PREFACE

This is a story of Victorian industrialists, entrepreneurs, and Edwardian grocers. The Britton, Moore, and Eastwood families have all seen several generations making iconic contributions to the industrial landscape of the United Kingdom. Their products have been sold around the world and can be seen in the homes of millions. This book is a social history of these families that discusses one of the world's most illustrious brands and reveals the true origins of the acronym "HP". Myths, rumours, and facts covering three centuries are now revealed after 120 years. The author, Nigel Britton, has researched intensively for several years, talking to family members and ancestors of those involved, and has now brought to the reader an in-depth story of those Victorian characters and their involvement with this world-famous condiment. He has tried to be open-minded as possible when dealing with speculation, myths, and rumour and to remain impartial despite having a personal interest in the subject, being the great-great-grandson of both Edward Eastwood the financier and Edwin Samson Moore, the Birmingham vinegar manufacturer who in 1899 turned a Nottingham-based local brown sauce into a British institution and a worldwide best seller.

The tentacles of these industrious families were to extend far and wide, spanning several generations and rubbing shoulders with prime ministers, famous railway and canal engineers, entrepreneurs, businessmen, philanthropists, stage, film, and television actors, television presenters, producers, artists, and celebrity chefs—and being associated with an infamous 1940s sex scandal and murder. They were to come in contact with a world-famous detective and one of the original Football League founders (now a regular Premiership club). Eventually, they would see their business enterprises valued for multi-millions.

> "Where does a family start? It starts with a young man falling in love with a girl. No superior alternative has yet been found."
>
> (Sir Winston Churchill)
> "The Churchill Years"

The Victorians were instrumental in the development of what we today know as a family. A love affair with business was equally thought of as the principal means of providing for future generations, whether that meant having the ambition to own a corner shop or a factory employing hundreds. The "family business" thrived in the Victorian period, with the Britton, Eastwood, and Moore families taking a prominent part in this era. Their business enterprises and products became household names during that time, and as such our story will begin with the author's immediate family, the "Brittons", of which the ancestors of author and his cousin, the TV celebrity Fern Britton, play a prominent part.

Although our title leads the reader to believe that this is a history of the world-famous condiment, which it is, it would be wrong not to acknowledge the author's ancestors, members of the Britton, Britain, Eastwood, and Moore families, who all grew up in the Victorian period in and around Birmingham and the industrial heartlands of the Midlands.

It's a BRITTON—British and Best *Illustration shows the "LION" Brass Cycle Inflator.*
Obtainable from (Reg. Trade Mark 545800) Drews Lane, Birmingham. 'Phone: East 0449. London Depot:
Cycle Dealers everywhere. CHAS. BRITTON LTD. (Est. 1881) 95, Pimlico Rd., S.W.1. (Stocks held) 'Phone: Sloane 6884.
Boxed Separately
1/5 EACH

Their business and enterprises of that period were of such importance that early chapters are given over to their history. These chapters will give the reader an insight not only on similar Victorian family businesses of that period but also on how ordinary, working-class men with good skills, training, and ambitions were able to use trade apprenticeships of their youth as stepping stones to go forward into business on their own.

The Victorian fashion for bicycles and the part played by the "Britton cycle pump", an invention by the business of the author's great-grandfather, Charles Britton, is also acknowledged.

Another invention of that decade also attributed to the Britton family was their hollow-cast process for toy soldiers, in particular, the world-famous "Britain's lead toy soldiers".

The Eastwood Carriage and Wagon Works Chesterfield would provide the finance for the joint enterprise of Edward Eastwood and his nephew Edwin Samson Moore's Midland Vinegar Company, who built their brewery at Aston Cross, Birmingham. They would later own HP Sauce.

The reader therefore will be at first introduced to the author's family and their contributions to the Victorian period of industry and commerce. The chapters that follow will outline the family connections and show how their finance would be instrumental in the establishment of the world-famous condiment HP Sauce and its history from 1874 to 2013.

(1)

"Britton" and "Britain": Who do you think you are?

For the budding genealogist, the phrase "Who do you think you are?" is a perpetual question born of a desire to understand their ancestors' lives, the circumstances they were born into, what made them the characters they were, and what influence they have had on subsequent generations.

Most of us know something about our own parents' early lives, and depending on which generation you were brought up in, probably as a child you were told snippets about your grandparents' and older family members' lives, experiences, and careers. Learning about their lives can go some way to making us understand why we are the people we seem to others and ourselves.

My parents were from Sutton Coldfield, Birmingham. They had moved to Cheshire before my birth, as my father had been studying at Manchester University. My father, like so many of his generation whose parents had run family businesses for decades, had chosen not to follow into his father's business. Instead, he heeded the calling of further education and university in particular as the place to strike out into the world.

By the 1950s, the Britton family had already been in business for over a century in several enterprises typical of the Victorians. They made their fortunes in Aston, Birmingham, which during the Industrial Revolution was known as the "City of a Thousand Trades". The Brittons had interests in spectacle frame manufacturing. They were gilt button makers, goldsmiths, silversmiths, watch makers, toy manufacturers, and pioneers in early photography. My great-grandfather Charles Britton was a brass founder.

Charles was born in 1852. His father, William Britton, was an optician and spectacle frame manufacturer from Birmingham. Charles did not follow in his father's career but was by training and profession a brass founder. By the end of the nineteenth century, he had made his fortune during the "cycle boom", making him one of Birmingham's most well-known and respected industrialists of the Victorian period.

The 1898 birth certificate of his youngest son, William Stanley, the author's grandfather, describes Charles as a "master brass founder". In 1878, Charles Britton married Elizabeth Lowry. Their union created nine children, two of whom enter our story: the author's grandfather, William Stanley, and his brother Edward Leslie.

Edward Leslie was the father of the actor and 1950-60s film star Tony Britton, who was born on 9 June, 1924, above the Trocadero public house in Temple Street, Birmingham. Leslie had entered the licence trade at an early age, having no interest in his father's bicycle pump manufacturing business. The Trocadero was and still is a well-known Birmingham city centre drinking and eating establishment.

Leslie's siblings frowned upon his career, which was thought of as not the most suitable profession for a son of a Victorian industrialist, never mind the right environment for bringing up a young child. Living above the Trocadero and city life had no detrimental effect on the young Tony, and until the age of eleven he attended the Edgbaston Collegiate School. With the family later moving to be licensees in Gloucestershire, Tony went to the Thornbury Grammar School.

In 1932, Leslie's father, Charles, died intestate. To solve the distribution of wealth and assets amongst the nine children, the cycle pump manufacturing business was bought out by Leslie's sister-in-law, Vera Eastwood.

With the Eastwood money, Leslie and his brother Wilfred were paid their share of the business, which was approximately £2000 (£110,000) each, as were Charles Ernest and James Percival, the elder sons. This was quite a considerable amount in the 1930s, especially if one considers the stock market crash and slump of that decade. Leslie's brother, the author's grandfather, William Stanley Britton, with his wife, Vera Eastwood's, finance, carried on with the cycle pump business with the remaining four sisters as directors.

With the outbreak of the Second World War, Leslie's family moved to Weston-Super-Mare to another licensed establishment. On Friday evenings in a corner of the pub, a small stage was erected, a place for local acts and those who thought they could sing, usually after several pints of Ansell's best bitter—early-day karaoke. Tony was allowed to stay up and sit at the top of the stairs watching the "turns", and these early exposures to entertainment would keep him in good stead when he later joined the Weston-Super-Mare amateur dramatics group and then turned professional, appearing on stage at the Old Vic and with the Royal

Shakespeare Company, all a very long way from the world of upstairs life at the Trocadero.

The distribution of the Charles Britton assets and business amongst the nine children caused quite a rift, which would see the family going in separate directions. Unfortunately for their children and future generations, this large family and their cousins have never been close, despite having total respect for one another's achievements, all of which have been followed over the decades with much interest, delight, and admiration.

Tony's career began at age eighteen, when the Weston-Super-Mare company staged *"Quiet Company"*. However, his future prospects were put on hold when in 1942 he joined the army. After the war he returned to the theatre, and his first job was as an assistant stage manager at the Manchester Library Theatre. There he learnt his trade and progressed to lead actor. He made his leading London debut in *"The Rising Wind"* at the Embassy Theatre. Other productions followed at London's Winter Gardens and the Edinburgh Festival.

Tony's career has been dominated by the theatre, but he has also appeared in over twenty films as lead and supporting actor, most notably *"There's a Girl in my Soup,"* Sunday Bloody Sunday, and The Day of the Jackal. His contributions to stage and film have also been equalled by his television appearances on popular favourites such as Robin's Nest, Don't Wait Up, and And Mother Makes Five, to name just a few. Tony and his first wife, Ruth (née Hawkins), have two children, the scriptwriter and producer Cherry Britton and the television presenter and author Fern Britton. Tony married for a second time to Danish sculptor and member of the wartime Danish resistance Eva Castle Britton (née Skytte Birkfeldt). They have one son, the actor Jasper Britton, who has followed in his father's footsteps with a career on stage, briefly interspersed with film and television appearances.

Fern, who is married to the television chef and presenter Phil Vickery, writes in her autobiography, *Fern Britton: My Story*, published in 2008, of her early childhood and separation from her father, Tony. Fern explains in her book how he remained a "glamorous if shadowy presence throughout my childhood" and it would be her mother and grandmother who would play a large part in her early life, with a paternal hand from her stepfather, George.

Much of Fern's early experiences and youth, including her time in drama college, her work as an assistant stage manager, and then her first TV job at Westward Television in Plymouth, are well documented in her autobiography. Suffice it to say that from her work as a continuity announcer at Westward TV in 1982 to the early days of the BBC breakfast show, I often saw my cousin on television. I knew who she was via our cousinship but was saddened that our families had been apart since those days of our great-grandfather's demise and the family rift caused by the inevitable disposal of his assets.

""There are only eighteen months between Fern and myself. I always thought our estrangement a shame for both of us, as during Fern's contract at Westward Television she had been living across the Tamar in Cornwall. During that same period I had also been living in the county. My parents' divorce early in the 1970s saw my mother and younger members of the family moving to Cornwall from Cheshire and living near St Ives, where I later married in 1982. I have watched both Tony's and Fern's stage, TV, and film careers from the side-lines with much admiration, and as such my knowledge of their lives and careers has been limited to the same as the reader.

Tony Britton's eldest child with his first wife, Ruth Hawkins, is Fern's sister Cherry. Cherry is a writer and producer who is married to the children's presenter Brian Cant, best known as the presenter of *Play School* and *Play-away*. He is also the much-acclaimed narrator of *Camberwick Green*, the delightful series followed by many children of the 1960s and 1970s. Cherry's stepson is the actor Richard Cant, who has been in several stage and television productions, most notably ITV's *Midsomer Murders*.

Without doubt I have been very lucky to find so many prominent members of my family involved with the stage, film, and television, and I am pleased to find that they have not been led astray into the "celebrity" lifestyle that is so apparent in the modern day. Perhaps that is because their careers have been established over decades; they have learnt their trade as theatrical tradition had dictated rather than through the now-so-familiar Saturday evening television diet of overnight fame.

Below: Tony Britton's Family Tree.

Charles Britton 1852-1932

Edward Leslie Britton 1894-1988
Nigel with "Great Uncle Leslie" at the
Nursing Home Weston-Super-Mare 1987

(Tony) Anthony Edward Lowry Britton. b1924

Below: Film, stage, and television actors,
Tony's Son, Daughters, and Step grandson,

Brian Cant—   *Richard Cant*   *Fern Britton—*   *Jasper Britton*
Cherry Britton   *Phil Vickery*

We return to our ancestors of the Victorian era, where we find Tony Britton's grandfather Charles Britton married to Elizabeth Margaret Lowry. Her ancestors were of Ulster descent, with family rumours that they were descended from the Earls of Munster.

Elizabeth's father, James Lowry, was born in Ulster in 1825. He was the captain and part-owner of one or more sailing ships. His business was not dissimilar to that depicted in the 1970s Sunday evening drama *The Onedin Line,* starring Peter Gilmore, a story of the daily lives of a shipping family trading from the port of Liverpool in the 1850s.

As in the *Onedin Line* drama, the Lowry shipping concern traded out of Liverpool and had its own tragedy when one of Captain James Lowry's ships was involved in a collision which saw his demise under tragic circumstances. James's wife, Mary, and son James Edward were also on board. Once the ship began to break up, the chief officer put James Edward and his mother aboard a lifeboat. Captain James Lowry, thinking they were still on board, went back to save them. The aft section sank, taking him with it. His wife was left a widow with five children to bring up. The final irony of it all was that to save money, Captain James Lowry had not insured his ship. Elizabeth Lowry overcame her father's death and moved with her family to Birmingham, where she met and married Charles Britton (1852-1932).

Charles had obviously been encouraged by his own father's endeavours. Born in 1820, William Britton was an optician and spectacle frame manufacturer from Vauxhall Street Aston, now the site of Aston University. William Britton's father, born in 1779, was also an industrious man, for we find him as a military ornament maker. His father, also called William, lived and worked in the 1790s at Freemason Street, Aston, as a gilt button maker. So Charles found himself with several skilled family members whom he must have looked up to, for we find him from a very early age training as a brass founder. His early career prospects took a dramatic upward turn when he was offered the position of works manager for a large firm in Birmingham, Benton and Stone Ltd. With his experience in brass founding, he did very well with the company, and it was not very long before he decided to set up his own business in the trade he knew so well. Charles, aged twenty-nine in 1881, established his business in a small factory in New Street Aston, Birmingham. Drawing on his knowledge of brass, he soon used this material in the manufacturer of his first range of insulators and pumps, which were taken up by the horticultural industries.

This was the principal business Charles Britton established, but his enterprise would expand rapidly with the invention in 1888 of the pneumatic tyre by John Boyd Dunlop (1840-1921). With the need to inflate this product, the Britton cycle pump was invented and went into full production.

John Boyd Dunlop studied to be a veterinary surgeon in Edinburgh and moved to Belfast in 1867. Roads at this time were poor, and wheels were protected by iron, wood, or solid rubber. During a moment of play with his son, Dunlop noticed how the boy was struggling with his tricycle, which had solid rubber tyres. Dunlop realised that a softer tyre would act as a shock absorber, making for a more comfortable ride and allowing better control of the wheel over the cobbles. Dunlop experimented with various bits of rubber and eventually found that if he wrapped the wheels of his son's tricycle with sheets of rubber and glued them together at the edges to make an air-tight seal, he was then able to inflate the constructed "tube" with a football pump. With this success he had invented the pneumatic tyre, which he patented in 1888. A year later, in 1889, he established a factory in Belfast and set about production. Two years later he moved to Birmingham and set up another factory at nearby Erdington, later known as "Fort Dunlop".

Charles Britton met with Dunlop, and the Britton Cycle pump was designed to complement the new pneumatic tyre. In 1896, Dunlop sold the company and transferred the patent to William Harvey Du Cros. Dunlop was given 1,500 shares in the new company and retired to Dublin. The company expanded in the next decade and became the multinational Dunlop Tire and Rubber Corporation and the Dunlop Rubber Co., Ltd.

John Boyd Dunlop 1840-1921

The Britton cycle pump was designed to complement Dunlop cycle tyres. Several million were produced, and cycles around the world carried a Britton pump fixed on their frame. The Britton pump was also manufactured for all the prominent cycle manufacturers and carried their names on the pump, usually accompanied by the "BRITTON" and "LION" trademarks.

The football pump John Boyd Dunlop had used to blow up his first experimental pneumatic tyre for his son's tricycle was a direct result of an invention two decades earlier, when Richard Lindon had introduced Indian rubber bladder inner-tubes to rugby balls.

Having had experience as a boot and shoe manufacturer close to the well re-known Rugby School, from which the game takes its name and also the novel "Tom Browns School Days" was based upon, Lindon had been called upon to produce an acceptable rugby ball. He made his balls for the School from hand-stitched, four-panel leather casings with an internal pig's bladder. It was reputed that the pig's bladder gave the ball its distinctive oval shape.

In those early years it was necessary to ask for volunteers to inflate the ball by blowing into the pig's bladder by inserting a clay pipe and using lung power. This was all done while the pig's bladder was still in its smelly "green" state. Richard Lindon's wife, the mother of his seventeen children, was called upon as one of those volunteers. It was said that while blowing up hundreds of those pig's bladders, which were most probably diseased, she contracted a fatal lung disease and died.

In 1850, vulcanised rubber was invented by an American, Charles Goodyear. Around 1862, Richard Lindon introduced the Indian rubber inner-tubes to rugby balls. Having been deeply affected by the presumed manner of his wife's death and knowing of the great difficulty of inflating a ball by mouth alone, Lindon invented the brass hand pump based on the design of the ordinary ear syringe. His invention was much acclaimed by all those, like himself, not wishing to use the former method of oral inflation.

Unfortunately, although he is credited with the invention of the rugby ball, the bladder, and the pump, Richard Lindon didn't patent them. By the 1880s there were several companies using his process for rugby balls, footballs, and several other industrial applications. Charles Britton was one of those entrepreneurs, and the Britton's were later to manufacture hand pumps for agriculture, cycle pumps for the cycle and motor cycle industry, and foot pumps for the motor car trade.

Above are shown Richard Lindon's 1875 brass hand syringe pump and the later invention of the foot pump, both of which Charles Britton manufactured on a large commercial scale.

With this rapid diversification into cycle pump manufacturing, the business of Charles Britton developed into a large concern. His New Street premises became a hive of high activity. His eldest son Charles Ernest became involved by the late 1890s. The business flourished, was mainly because of the cycle boom of that decade, which would see the Brittons manufacturing hundreds of thousands of cycle pumps.

The firm moved to larger premises in 1898 at Theodore Street, Aston Newtown, where the business expanded again. With the death of Queen Victoria in 1901, the Edwardian era had arrived, and with it the demand for individual bicycles, motor cycles, and motor car accessories. Throughout the Britton's history, the companies had always been involved in the production of cycle pumps and electrical products, where they were pioneers well before the Lucas empire.

Charles Ernest was an inventive man and was as skilled in the use of hand tools as his father. He was fascinated by electrical gadgets and made his first motor cycle himself in the early 1900s. He built his own ignition coil at home, wound it, and used some of his mother's kitchen equipment and the cooking range hob to melt and run wax as insulation.

Charles Ernest, however, was far from content working with his father, and he soon decided to make a break in 1908 from the business and set up on his own account in a small building in Stanisforth Street, Aston. This was partly possible with the financial help of his father-in-law, Edgar Canning. The "Canning Empire" had been established by an ancestor, William Canning, in 1785 and was a large industrial concern in the Midlands, the country, and the world at large well into the twentieth century.

Charles Ernest's small workshop was operating next door to an equally ambitious young man, R. T. Shelly, later to found R. T. Shelley, Ltd., who later became managing director of Norton Motors, Ltd., motor cycle manufacturers whose international fame rested on their success in the Isle of Man TT and Grand Prix races. Charles Ernest friendship with R. T. Shelly would later see the Britton's responsible for the design and development of a motor cycle pump specifically for all Norton machines.

Charles Ernest soon found, like so many new business enterprises, that early success could not be guaranteed even with well-known family members associated to the trade. He soon came in trouble with his raw material supplies. It is reputed that his father, Charles Sr, had been to see the suppliers, making it known to them that it was no longer possible to supply himself and his son now that they were in business as competitors.

Charles Britton was well known throughout the cycle trade and had been a good customer for many years. The suppliers, not wishing him to take his trade elsewhere, halted all supplies to Charles Ernest. Samaritan-like, in 1909 Ernest re-joined his father. Perhaps it was with the promise that because of age, Charles Britton was soon to retire, that made his son return. And so it was in 1912 and after the death of his wife, Elizabeth Britton. Charles indeed retired, and Ernest took over the immediate running of the business. By this time Charles Ernest's younger brother James Percival had also joined the firm, and from this period onwards, the two brothers ran their father's business. Charles Ernest developed the electrical side of the business while James Percival handled the day-to-day administration of the company.

New materials were developing all the time, and an alternative to metal for bicycle pumps emerged with the production of celluloid. Celluloid was the first man-made plastic material, invented in 1865 by a Birmingham man, Parks. Parks was trying to discover a substitute for paper maché, experimenting with various combinations of acids and alkalis with cellulose pulp, when he accidentally added camphor. Parks took out a patent on his process but never actually produced what he called Parksene in commercial quantities. It was taken up by the Americans, who produced it industrially, and later by British Xylonite, later known as BXL Ltd.

Celluloid became a very important material, and its uses were taken up by the firm Dover Limited, a company in the pump making business. They were making, straightening, and smoothing celluloid tube in the early 1900s, and Charles Ernest, who was a friend of the Dover brothers, bought all his materials from them. The Britton pumps were now being made with celluloid, and they were producing pumps for cycle and motor cycle companies across the country. One of their main customers was Dunlop, who were being supplied with orders of two and three hundred thousand pumps at any one time. Dunlop's pumps were always wrapped in a yellow packet with a picture of its founder, John Boyd Dunlop, on them.

Dunlop was a bearded gentlemen, and the Indian market was delighted to see his picture on the box, as many of their purchasers thought it was Jesus Christ. They insisted on the yellow box with his image, which only went to increase sales for Dunlop and the Britton pump, which was now being sold to all the far reaches of the globe.

English-made celluloid pumps were an instant success. Exports to the continent were very strong, particularly in France, where they were looked upon as a great novelty. In 1913, however, the French manufacturers complained about the Britton pumps under-cutting them, and subsequently extra tariffs were put on all British-made bicycle products by the French government.

To overcome the French tariffs, Charles Britton and his son Charles Ernest decided that they would set up a branch factory in Paris. This was to avoid import duties by shipping components to the French factory duty-free and assembling there. Charles Ernest went over to France and managed the factory for several years. The French were to soon extend their import duties to cover components, and it soon became difficult to find raw materials locally at competitive prices. All this continued until war broke out in 1914. The Britton's agent, who had been with them before they set up the branch factory in Paris, remained there as sales manager.

The Britton's French agent, Monsieur Beauxden, continued to make sales as best he could. This went on with supplies being difficult to obtain until 1915, when the English representative of the German firm of Managmen came to see Charles Ernest. The Brittons bought large quantities of brass and steel from them in addition to the tube already being bought from Kynock, one of the original firms who were later to evolve as ICI. The English representative of Managmen explained to Charles Ernest that he was in some difficulty because his German firm had always kept considerable stocks of tube in a London warehouse, from which the English firms who used tube for the various trades were able to get their supplies.

When war broke out, all transactions were frozen. The representative was now in some difficulty, as 50 per cent of his salary was from commission, which was quite considerable. As the German stock was frozen, he was losing potential income. So he offered Charles Ernest what would have been his commission on the materials in exchange for releasing the supplies in the warehouse. Charles Ernest was more than happy with the offer and readily agreed. The Brittons must have held quite a lot of respect and influence, for permission was granted from the Board of Trade, which was in control of such matters. They released the materials, which was a great help to the representative.

Some time later, the representative of the German firm came to see Charles Ernest to express his gratitude and make him an advantageous offer. Because of his association with the steel companies of Germany, he happened to know about the steel formulation in the manufacturer of magnets. Up until the outbreak of war, Bosh were the main suppliers of magnets to this country, with imports coming from the Bosh factory direct from Germany. The Bosh magnets were much more reliable than the British ones, which were made at that time by CAV, Lucas, Rotax, and Miller. These magnets were required for the "Magnetos", which produced the spark to the sparking plugs and were later replaced by coil ignition.

The representative revealed to Charles Ernest that the Admiralty were having problems with the manufacturer of magnets for their sea and other plane engines. The failure rate of these magnets was quite high. The representative, through his knowledge of German steel, had come to the conclusion that this was due to the steel not having a good formulation. He had been approached by the Admiralty, who had asked him if he could put them in contact with anyone who could produce magnets. This, then, was why the representative had decided to approach Charles Ernest.

Charles Ernest had been at school with a man who was now a Professor of Metallurgy at Birmingham University, so he got in touch with him and asked how he should proceed. The professor replied that any problems could be overcome and recommended to him the firm of Neil of Sheffield, who gave the necessary technical assistance. The Brittons went into the manufacturing of these and other magnets, and by the end of the war they were producing them in large quantities and very successfully. Financially they did very well out of it, although initially it did involve a considerable amount of capital outlay for plant. The Brittons' Magnetos had many applications during the war. They were used in the ignition systems of spark-ignition piston engines. Planes, motor cycles, and cars all benefited from these magnetos in their products. The Brittons soon found they were being sought after by many manufacturers, which made Charles Britton into one of the well-known Birmingham industrialists of his day.

During the First World War, cycle pumps would still play a large part of the business, with the introduction of the folding bicycle for troops manufactured by BSA; Birmingham Small Arms Company, situated at Small Heath, Birmingham. Britton designed a small cycle pump especially for its use. After the war the business continued its success with the manufacture of permanent magnets for motor cycles, cars, and aircraft supplied to the firms of CAP, ML, BTH, ELC, and Thompson and Bennett, which became known as Lucas. However with the end of the war, orders for aircraft from the ministry dropped. The coil ignition became more widely used, and the manufacture of magnets was reduced. The bicycle pump side of the business was once again resumed and built up. Another change of address came with the move to even larger premises at Drews Lane, Ward End, Birmingham, right next door to the Riley Motor Car Company. At these new premises, the Brittons continued with the pump business but also began to make telephone magnets. With the advent of the moving-coil loudspeaker, they concentrated on this business for the principal radio manufacturers.

A magneto is an electrical generator that uses permanent magnets to produce periodic pulses of alternating current. The cycle industry Charles Britton knew so well soon used them to power lights on bicycles. These were more commonly known as a dynamo, and when in contact with the wheel as it was turning, they generated enough power to illuminate the front and back lights. This provided immediate safety for cycling during the dark hours of the day. The Brittons produced hundreds of thousands of magnetos, and many were used in the manufacture of "Bottle" dynamos for the cycle industry.

Another use of magnetos was in the early manual telephones, which used a hand-cranked magneto generator to produce a relatively high-voltage alternating signal to ring the bells of other telephones on the same party line and to alert the operator. These were usually on long rural lines served by small manual exchanges, which were not "common battery". The telephone instrument was "local battery", containing two large zinc dry cells.

**BRITTON'S PUMPS
—BRITISH AND BEST**

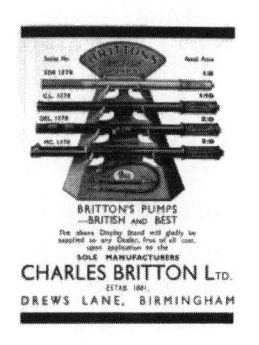

SOLE MANUFACTURERS
CHARLES BRITTON L<small>TD.</small>
ESTAB. 1881
DREWS LANE, BIRMINGHAM

Stands for selling Britton's cycle pumps were given free to the cycle outlets.

With his elder sons in charge and running the business successfully, Charles Britton retired to his beloved Melrose House on Sutton Road, Erdington, alongside the Eastwood and Moore residences. Melrose was a grand residence in two and half acres with tennis courts, a paddock, and a stabling block with a garage that housed the family's 1912 Rover car. The property had large living and domestic accommodation, with gardeners, maids, and a cook. The family chauffer, "Gibbs", complemented the staff. The garden had around one hundred fruit trees, including apple, plum, and pear, and a variety of fruit bushes. There were two large greenhouses with mature vines giving an abundance of grapes.

While Charles Ernest and James Percival were busy expanding the Britton empire, Ethel Britton, one of Charles Britton's daughters who never married, looked after the general running of the home. She had been in over-all charge as housekeeper for Charles ever since her mother, Elizabeth, had died in 1912. With the end of hostilities in 1919, many of those who had previously worked in domestic service and who had been called upon to work on farms and in the factories while their men folk went to France decided that the pay and conditions of domestic service were no longer viable in comparison. The Brittons still managed to keep on daily help, but with the children now adults and beginning to live away from home, Ethel's role diminished.

The author recalls an amusing story told to him by Edward Leslie Britton in 1988 on a visit to the Western-Super-Mare nursing home, where Leslie spent his last years. He was in his ninety-fourth year, and during his reminiscence of the "Pump Brittons", he told of an episode when he had taken a day off work as the licensee of a Birmingham pub. For months he had told one of his regulars, George, all about his family, who by now were known as the "Pump Brittons of Sutton Coldfield", a term used to distinguish them from the area's Britton goldsmiths and Britain toymakers. Leslie had enthused about their large business interests and the "mansion" home of his father along the Sutton Road Erdington, which was still a rural retreat in the 1920s with none of the suburbia spread there is today.

"One day," he had told George, "I will take you up there for afternoon tea with my sister Ethel." So on this particular day, Leslie, with his pub regular, advanced on Melrose House with eager expectations.

Melrose House, the Brittons' once commodious residence on the Sutton Road, Erdington. The grounds having been more or less cleared by the time of this late-1950s photo, the site was made ready for demolition prior to the building of the infamous Lyndhurst Estate.

Leslie and George entered Melrose by the rear kitchen door, for his sister Ethel would not entertain anyone by the front of the house unless by previous appointment. She was your 1920s version of Mrs Bouquet from *Keeping up Appearances*, the BBC Sunday evening sit-com. Ethel ushered her brother and his friend George hurriedly into the kitchen and offered them tea and cake. George the pub regular was a typical hard-working "Brummie", the salt of the earth kind with a strong, deep, West Midlands accent straight from the Black Country. After tea and cake had been taken with only the slightest interruption for polite conversation, Ethel enquired whether they had enjoyed their tea. Before Leslie could give his thanks, George stepped up with "thut wer luvlies missus a smashin cuppa tea". Ethel's face, said Leslie, was a picture. She found it impossible to hide her initial surprise and distaste, having never associated with anyone but her chums from the gin and tonic set at the Sutton Coldfield golf club. For her to hear a working-class voice, and in her own home, was something to see, said Leslie. Another story Leslie recalled was when he took his then young son, Tony, to see Ethel at Melrose House. Leslie had some business in nearby Erdington that day and asked Ethel to look after Tony. Tony was taken to the library, where he was left alone for nearly three hours. Eventually he got up and left. Although only eight years old at the time, he managed to find his own way along the Sutton Road and back to Birmingham. Perhaps Ethel thought, as did some middle-class Edwardians, that "children should be seen and not heard" and Tony would entertain himself in the library.

A glorious, sunny, tree-lined Sutton Road, where the Britton, Moore, and Eastwood families all had desirable residences in the Victorian and Edwardian period. Notice the neatly clipped privet hedges, trees, and bushes. These grand houses were demolished around 1956, and large tower-block housing association estates have replaced them.

Holly Lane Erdington at the junction of the Sutton Road. The Brittons home, Melrose House, and Edwin Samson Moore's York Lodge were built directly opposite this junction at No.'s 62 and 66, Sutton Road.

It's a BRITTON—British and Best
CHAS. BRITTON LTD.
1/5 EACH

Charles Britton Senior died in 1932 intestate. It appears he had refused to face up to the problem of making a will, not knowing how to dispose of the assets amongst his nine children. This caused quite a family rift amongst the brothers and sisters. Charles Ernest and James Percival believed they should take over the business with perhaps one or other siblings being a director. This was refused by the majority, who believed that all the siblings should have directorships. For Charles and his brother James, this was not acceptable. They believed as they had been the ones who had developed the business for many years, unlike the younger members of the family, they should be the main directors. If all the siblings were made directors, Charles and James could be outvoted by the others at any meeting, so it was left to the banks to hold an auction between the two sides.

It's a BRITTON—British and Best
CHAS. BRITTON LTD.
2/- EACH

William Stanley Britton, the author's grandfather, had the good fortune to marry Vera Eastwood. Vera was the granddaughter of Edward Eastwood and Edwin Samson Moore, whose Midland Vinegar Company and purchase of HP Sauce had ensured that later generations would be financially taken care of. As our story unfolds, these gentlemen take a prominent part. Vera was able to raise the sufficient funds, approximately three-quarters of a million pounds in 2013 terms, to buy out the business on behalf of her husband, Stanley Britton, and his four sisters and two brothers, Edward Leslie and Wilfred.

William "Stanley" Britton and Vera Josephine Britton née Eastwood Marion Esther Eastwood née Moore Circa 1955

Within a year, Edward and Wilfred had expressed no more interest with the business, and Vera Eastwood bought out their shares, leaving her husband and his sisters in sole ownership.

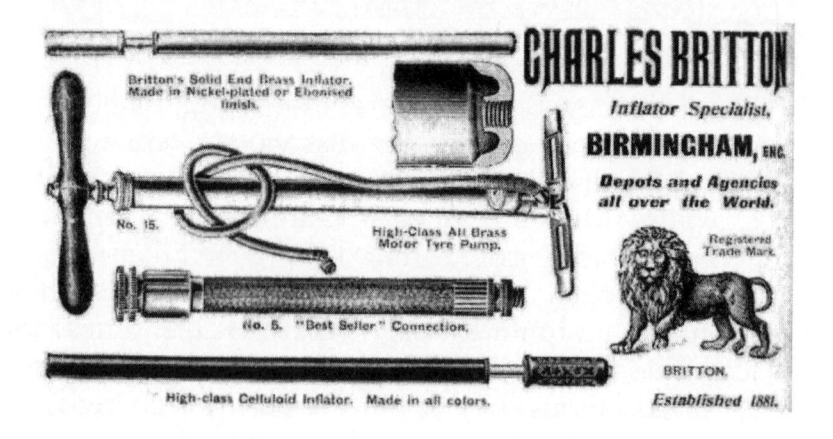

Vera Eastwood, the author's grandmother, financed the purchase of her late father-in-law's business from Barclays

Bank in 1932. They acted as vendors on behalf of the estate of Charles Britton Cycle Pump and Magnet Manufacturer at Ward End Works, Drews Lane, near Birmingham.

With Vera Eastwood's finance enabling a speedy solution to the division of Charles Britton's cycle pump business, Charles Ernest and James Percival set up their own company as C. E. & J. P. Britton, Ltd., and expanded it into a large concern at Witton, Birmingham. Family rumour held that prior to the death of Charles Britton, the two brothers had already planned an exit strategy, knowing that their father's lack of a will made possible friction amongst the family and problems of the ownership of the future business. Charles and James had already leased the Witton factory and had taken various plant and production machinery from the Ward End business as a fall-back position in case, as suspected, there would be problems with the distribution of Charles Britton's business assets.

It would therefore be a bold and brave step of William Britton, who had only brief experience of his father and elder brothers business and had been more as a spectator than anything, to take that leap of faith and, with the moral and financial backing of his wife, became the managing director of Charles Britton, Ltd. He continued with the cycle pump and mudguard side of the business well into the late 1960s at the Ward End factory.

Over the years, land surrounding the works was sold off to property speculators. Stanley's sisters preferred more from their directors' income than investing in new plant and machinery, and the author's father had no interest in the business. It was sold to Bantel, makers of children's toy scooters. This brought to an end over eighty years of Britton cycle pump manufacturing.

During the 1932 purchase of the Britton manufacturing business, there was a court case between the two companies of Charles Britton Limited and C. E. & J. P. Britton Limited over the trade name "BRITTON". William Stanley Britton, the new managing director of Charles Britton Limited, won the case and continued to use the trade name "BRITTON" on all his company's products. C. E. & J. P. Britton registered the name "BRITANNIA" for their products. This court case didn't help relationships between the two sides of the family, and later generations would be estranged from their cousins as a result.

C. E. & J. P. Britton Limited went on to develop their business into a large concern at Witton, Birmingham, manufacturing cycle pumps, mudguards and magnets. After the Second World War, they developed new products for the building trade: the country's first domestic cold water tanks in high-density polythene. These were designed to fit into the lofts of homes and waste water systems, such as for kitchen and bathroom waste. The company went out of the Britton family in the late 1970s.

Our story must now leave the industrious Britton family of the author. Their legacy is now part of the British cycle history, and their film, stage, and television productions have been seen on stage, in cinemas, and in millions of homes nationwide and are now firmly established within the history of the British film and entertainment world.

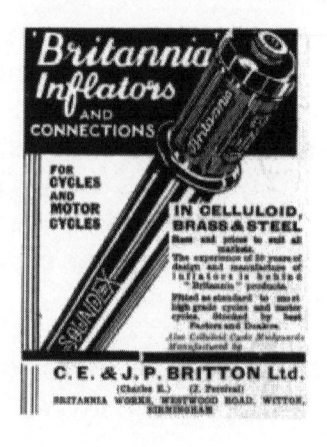

Charles Britton set up his brass founding business in a small factory in New Street, Birmingham, during the early 1880s.

Bottom row, third from left: Mr Edgar Canning and Mrs Canning, Mr Streather and Mrs Streather, Norman Britton, Vera Streather, Groom, Clifford Streather, Bride, Enid Britton. Centre Row: Tenth from left, William Stanley Britton (the author's grandfather).

The splendour and grandeur of the grounds of "Melrose House" provided an ideal setting for the wedding reception of Enid Britton and Clifford Streather.

The wedding of Enid Britton to Clifford Streather, July 1928. Enid was the daughter of Charles Ernest Britton and Minnie Britton née Canning

Bottom row, right to left: Aunt Bell Long née Lowry, Lillian Sutherland née Britton, Charles Britton Snr., Minnie Britton née Canning, Charles Ernest Britton.

Middle row: Second right, Doris Monks née Britton, fifth right Vera Josephine Eastwood (the author's grandmother), seventh right Edward Leslie Britton, Kate Britton née Richardson, James Percival Britton.

Top row right to left: Ethel Britton, Mabel Allday née Britton.

In 2003 Fern Britton was presenting the ITV *This Morning* daytime programme with Philip Scholfield. During one of the daily topics of interest, the subject of family history and genealogy was given a part. A guest expert on the programme was asked to research both the presenters' family history.

Anthony Adolp, one of the country's leading genealogists, carried out a thorough investigation into the Britton ancestors of Fern. Much was already known to the author, so it wasn't a surprise to find evidence of past Brittons' achievements. This programme didn't let us down in understanding how other Brittons had aspired to greater things.

Genealogists know that whilst researching family members, it's not unusual to come across surnames that have been misspelt. Anthony Adolph explained that when giving details of a new-born child's name to the local records office, surnames were spelt at the direction of the officer taking down the details. Also, when there was a census, the recording officer often wrote names as they interpreted them. Thus, we often find surnames with slightly different spellings.

The grandson of William Britton the gilt button maker had his name written as Britain rather than Britton. There is family speculation that this was deliberately done to distinguish this side of the family from the other Brittons in and around Birmingham and Aston, who were involved during the nineteenth century in all kinds of new inventions and concerns. Apart from the Britton cycle pump business, there were also Britton goldsmiths, jewellers, spectacle frame manufacturers, and watch makers. The Brittons were indeed an industrious family and Charles Britton's 2nd Cousin, William Britain [1828-1906] was no different.

The firm of Britains Ltd was established by William Britain in Birmingham about 1845. Not much is known about his early life except that he was a brass finisher, brass cock maker, and mechanical toy maker. We have no record as to why he moved to North London from Birmingham, but he soon set up a small but successful business making toys during the 1850s at his home at 28 Lambton Road, Hornsey Rise, Northeast London. The toy trade had been dominated by the European continent throughout this century, but

William Britain gradually established a cottage industry involving the whole family, producing ingenious mechanical clockwork toys. These were too expensive to be mass produced but gave the Britains a modest income.

William's business soon flourished, mainly through his hard work, and he was joined by his sons, William Junior and Dennis. The Britain family made a formidable team who set about producing various toy products. With much competition from abroad, the Britains soon realised that they would have to come up with a more competitive and advantageous product that could position them higher in the marketplace over their rivals.

During this latter part of the Victorian era and with the new middle class becoming well established across the country, mass-marketed toys soon became available to those with more disposable income. The Victorian Christmas was now enjoyed and celebrated by the giving of small gifts to and from adults, and their children would enjoy the delights of the toy manufacturers' latest designs. The Britains soon realised that toy soldiers imported from Germany seemed to be very popular. These were solid and quite expensive, and Britain's decided that a cheaper manufactured version would have equal if not greater success by making the price achievable to even more of the middle-class population.

William Britain Junior (1860-1933) had joined the family business as a young man, and after much experimentation he designed the hollow casting process for manufacturing toy soldiers. This process was totally revolutionary and gave the Britain family the competitive edge they had been seeking over their rivals.

This major development for the company occurred in 1893, with William Britain Junior finding a way of casting lead figures that were hollow, more lifelike, and, most importantly, more economical than the two-dimensional, solid figures known as "flats" that had been made by German toy manufacturers. The first Britain's set was of mounted Life Guards. Britain's experimented with new ideas, and in 1896 figures with movable arms were introduced. This involved a separate casting with a loop at the shoulder end that slipped over a stud-like projection. Moveable arms provided better "play value" for children but also led to lose arms, which became detached. In the 1930s it became possible for new replacement arms to be purchased directly from toy shops.

William Junior designed and cut all the models for toy soldiers, which at first were quite crude and often incorrectly proportioned. However, they rapidly improved with every new model released. This, together with new painting techniques, saw the company become renowned for its hollow-cast lead toys, which were well-researched to ensure accuracy of uniforms and arms. By 1900 the company had produced over a hundred different sets.

The method of commercially producing the hollow-cast soldiers involved pouring the molten metal into hinged brass moulds by hand. The metal was an alloy, a mixture of lead, tin, and antinomy. As it cooled, the alloy formed a skin around the shape inside the mould. The mould was then turned upside down, and the residue metal streamed out through a funnel in the mould. Air holes were left at strategic points to make sure that metal reached the extremities of the mould. The thinner parts of the model, such as horses' legs and rifle barrels, were left solid to prevent breakages. Skilled operators could produce up to three hundred castings per hour.

The size and scale of toy soldiers were based on the scale of the then most popular size of toy trains, 1 gauge. The soldiers were 54 mm (2 1/8 inches) tall, and this has since been referred to as the Standard Scale. At first, Britain's made regiments from the United Kingdom, including mounted Life Guards, the household cavalry of the queen, foot soldiers, and guardsmen.

William's younger brother Frederick became the salesman of the family and set out to convince the conservative-minded British store owners that Britain's lead soldiers were worthy of being sold alongside the German Heyde figures made in Dresden and the French Mignot pieces made in Paris. Initially business was slow due to these imports, but the expansion of the British Empire in the later decades of the nineteenth century resulted in a larger Royal Navy and British Army with new battalions.

The company then developed a new series based on contemporary events, and in 1897 model troops of the Empire began to appear, celebrating Queen Victoria's Diamond Jubilee.

Britain's opened an office in Paris in 1905, and models were adapted for the French market. British royal and ceremonial occasions, such as the accession to the British throne, coronations, and trooping the colour, provided an opportunity to issue souvenir and ceremonial lines connected with the royal family. Britain's became a limited company on 4 December 1907, and the new board of directors included William Britain Junior, Alfred Britain, Fredrick Britain, Edward Britain, and Frank Britain. Like other companies in 1914, they were encouraged by the British government to produce toys of a patriotic nature, so cannon on gun carriages and soldiers poised for battle joined the range of model soldiers.

The 1920s saw a dramatic change in Britain's product range. The company introduced U. S. Army and Navy figures as well as South American soldiers and Canadian Mounties, but sales plummeted due to the rejection of military-style war toys after the carnage of the First World War. Britain's responded by introducing a farm, zoo, and circus series.

Production at Britain's went from strength to strength. Extensions to the house next door at Lambton Road, Hornsey Rise, eventually culminated in the whole block being torn down and a factory, warehouse, and office complex established with some three hundred workers. Eventually another factory, known as the North Light Building, was constructed at Walthamstow, also in Northeast London, where the Britain's Model Home Farms production was moved to in 1931.

Beginning in 1897 or 1898, each box set was numbered. By the time the Model Home Farms series was launched in 1923, the military sets were up to No. 250. The sets ranged from a standard single row of eight infantrymen or five cavalry to the top-of-the-range Set No. 131, with 275 pieces.

From 1900, Britain's toy soldiers were signed and given the date the master figure was made, either under the base of the figure or belly of the horse. This was done to protect the firm against design piracy from competitors.

Initially paper labels were attached, but later details were embossed into the bases. Dating continued until the Copyright Act of 1911 was introduced, after which it was only necessary to provide the maker's name. However, some figures with dates were made well into the 1920s before new moulds were put into production. Zinc alloy models made after the Second World War had no lettering on their bases.

The Britain's company prepared its own paint pigments, and staff painted all the figures. Only after the Second World War did the firm begin using outside paint suppliers and outworkers for painting. The first types of paint probably contained less varnish, so earlier model soldiers have a matte finish. Until 1902, only rifle butts were painted a brown colour, and the rest was left as bare metal. Swords were never painted silver but also left as bare metal.

During the 1930s, Britain's survived the economic depression by developing every money-generating product it could think of. New types of model proliferated: zoos, gardens, circuses, and motor vehicles were produced. The 1940 range, marketed just before the company had to go over to war production, was the largest ever. The return to normality after the Second World War was slow, and it was not until 1953 that a reasonable range was offered. Box labels were standardised to a single "All Nations" design. Almost immediately, plastic began to pose a serious threat. By the mid-1960s it had almost entirely taken over, and in 1966 the era of the hollow cast toy soldier finally came to an end, although not before some 1,000 million had been manufactured. In 1959, Herald, the leading manufacturer of plastic toy soldiers, was acquired by Britains and with it considerable expertise in the new material.

Britain's began as a family company and remained so for decades. The company was sold for the first time in 1984, when Dennis Britain decided to retire. W. Britain was sold to The Dobson Park Group. The company changed hands many times over the next twenty years, going from Dobson to Ertl to Racing Champions and finally to First Gear. First Gear owns W. Britain today.

W. Britain has gone through a number of changes over the years in manufacturing styles, products, and ownership. However, the quality of their toy soldiers and farm animals has been maintained and improved over more than a hundred years of production.

I first came across Britain's Toys as a child in the 1960s. Having the good fortune of being born in January, I received my Christmas and birthday money at the same time of year. My grandmother, Vera Eastwood, always sent my cards with four brand-new, crisp, green one-pound notes, two for Christmas and two for my birthday. It was a rare treat to go into the local toy shop, "Bunty's", in Bramhall Village and spend what seemed to me a small fortune on Britain's Toys.

I was given the Britain's Toy Farm as a present. I remember as a seven-year-old peering in wonder though the glass display cabinets at the cows, goats, sheep, and all manner of farm animals, tractors, trailers, and farm implements, which all gave a young boy a huge choice of what to add to his collection. My youngest brother had the zoo and my elder brother a fort and soldiers. "Dinky" and "Corgi" toy cars, stamp collecting, and "Britain's" were the staple diet of boys growing up in those post-war years.

Throughout the sixties, seventies, and eighties, the success of the Britains continued, and the brand name was prominently established. Its range of plastic farm animals and complementary die cast vehicles are worthy upholders of the standards and now expected to satisfy the expanding collectors' market.

So William Britain, an enterprising young man from Birmingham, travelled to London in the mid-1850s and transformed his business from a small cottage industry to a multinational enterprise. His was a typical reward for those Victorian values of family, enterprise, and hard work.

William Britain

William Britain Jnr.

Dennis Britain

(2)

Vinegar and Spice

Born just three years earlier than Charles Britton, the master brass founder, was the author's great-great-grandfather Edwin Samson Moore, who entered the industrious Victorian era on 5 April, 1849, in Newcastle-under-Lyme, Staffordshire.

His father was Jacob Moore (1822) from Lee Bank, Birmingham, a highly skilled man who started his business career as a tool maker at 7 Newhall Street in the heart of Birmingham's "City of a Thousand Trades". Jacob moved to Newcastle-under-Lyme, Staffordshire, where he established a printing business and where he met and married Louisa Limer Moore, apparently no relation. Tragedy befell the Moore's, with Louisa dying in childbirth. Soon after, Jacob remarried and returned to Birmingham. Jacob continued his career and soon had a thriving lithographic and printing business at 11/12 Broad Street, as described by a local trade directory of 1890.

Samson had not joined his father in the family business. However, by this date Jacob would have been sixty-eight years old. His youngest son, George Lloyd Moore, from his third marriage, had been involved in his father's photography business for several years and was also by then a pioneer with early photography. His partnership with Charles Howell and Frank James Smith and their Midland Camera Company traded from Slaney Street, Birmingham, as photographic apparatus manufacturers.

English Field Camera: 1905-11. The Midland Camera Company of Slaney Street, Birmingham, added "Ltd." to their title in 1905. However, they went into liquidation in 1911. Labelled with the "Ltd." addendum, this example of their work has to be between these two dates. It is very advanced for its time. It has gearing to the rising and cross-front shift movements, and to the back, which can be wound forward for wide-angle work. All corners are cross-banded in ebony inlay. This was not a cheap camera at the time it was made.

On the next page: A catalogue of the Midland Camera Company's photographic and apparatus products.

In 1902, one of the three partners, Frank James Smith, left the Midland Camera Company. Charles Howell and George Lloyd Moore remained, but in 1912 the company was wound up. The trademarks and possibly the remaining stock and business were passed to Thornton Pickard, a well-established camera manufacturer from Manchester.

George Lloyd Moore leaves our story. Of the other members of the Moore family, Jacob Moore's sister Abigail Moore (1827-1903) married Edward Eastwood ((Edwin Samson's uncle)), who plays an important part in their joint venture later in our story). Jacob and Abigail's father, Isaac Moore (1792), was a toy manufacturer married to Sarah Millington. Jacob's wife, Louisa, was from Newcastle-under-Lyme, and her father, Charles Moore, was a timber dealer from Lee Bank, Birmingham.

Edwin Samson Moore did not follow his father into the printing business. Instead, Samson set his sights in a different direction. He started his early career as a Birmingham representative of W. Pink & Sons of Portsmouth, "Pinks Pickles". Other family members of this large concern traded as E & T Pickles, founded in the late 1880s in Bermondsey, South London. We look at the Pinks concerns later in our story. However, Pinks Pickles were importers and suppliers of pickles and spices. Edwin Samson obviously took to this new career. He immersed himself in knowledge of all Pinks products and soon realised how profitable this business was.

We soon find him in partnership as a commission agent. The following notice takes this up.

The London Gazette, 22 December, 1871

"Notice is hereby given, that the Partnership hereto-fore subsisting between us the undersigned, Henry Strange and Edwin Samson Moore, as Commission Agents, of 7, Lee-Crescent, Birmingham, in the county of Warwick, under the style of Strange and Moore, was dissolved on the 7th day of March last by mutual consent—Dated this 14th day of December, 1871." Henry Strange Edwin Samson Moore.

Lee Crescent, Edgbaston, Birmingham, photograph taken in 1964. These "modest" middle-class Regency-style houses date from the 1830s. It's the author's theory that Samson Moore was using the family home as his registered office. Henry Strange, one presumes, was an equally young enthusiastic young man of approximately the same age as Samson who had decided early on in their partnership that a commission agent wasn't going to be his future career.

Edwin Samson Moore was twenty-two years old at the date of the London Gazette notice. The notice gives the reader an insight into his early business life. His brief partnership with Henry Strange sees them trading as commission agents, which leads us to believe that Samson was in fact an agent or representative for W. Pink & Sons rather than an employee of theirs. Samson is also noted as a representative for the Cambrian Vinegar Company, Elland Road, Leeds. They produced vinegar, black beer, and spruce beer.

Black beer can trace its roots back as far as 1555, when it began as "spruce beer", which was produced by mashing and fermenting the leaves of spruce pine. In 1769, Captain Cook, the great Yorkshire explorer, started brewing black beer and gave it to his sailors to ward off scurvy on their Australasian adventures.

Allegedly a health-giving brew, black beer is taken, not drunk, for its perceived medical and nutritional benefits, notably its high vitamin C content. It is not sipped neat but diluted with lemonade or milk. When mixed with the former it becomes "Sheffield Stout" and tastes like a malty cross between dandelion and burdock and bitter shandy, with a faint caramel kick.

Black beer can still be found today behind the bar in almost every Yorkshire pub, usually nestled beside a dusty bottle of Stone's Green Ginger Wine.

So for the next three years this would be Samson's main source of income. Whether he was self-employed or an employee, records do not show. However, a new branch of the Cambrian Brewery was established in Birmingham, and Samson Moore was asked to set it up.

The Cambrian Vinegar Company, Elland Road, Leeds

Samson Moore soon found his vast experience invaluable to the Cambrian Vinegar Company, where he was instrumental in establishing their branch in Birmingham. Although that was only a small brewery for malt vinegar, Samson relished the responsibility given to him. By the time he was twenty-five, vinegar was literally flowing through his veins. Edwin Samson Moore was also a representative of Pinks Pickles of Portsmouth, selling their products in and around the Midlands, an association that a quarter of a century later would prove to be invaluable.

The Moore and Eastwood families had by now been involved in many of the main industries of the nineteenth century. By 1874, Samson's uncle, Edward Eastwood, had a thriving railway carriage and wagon business in Chesterfield. Their families had followed one another's business ramifications over the years, and Samson would have taken great interest in not only his father's and grandfather's businesses but also his uncle's.

Samson, who had close-hand experience of vinegar brewing and production from the establishment of the Cambrian Vinegar Company Leeds branch at Birmingham combined with his sales experience and knowledge of related products for Pinks Pickles, thought that surely he could do worse than set himself up in a similar vein.

Samson had married Mary Payne in 1871. They had already started a family, and Mary was expecting again. Samson knew the time was right for his own venture with the added incentive of providing for his family's future prosperity. He had made a comfortable home in Hunters Vale, Hockley Hill, for his family. When his first son was a day old, he decided on a brisk walk towards Aston Cross via the ever-increasing streets of Aston New Town. As he walked around this new industrial landscape, he surveyed the availability of land for any possible business venture. It wasn't long before he came across a large hoarding newly erected on land that was being advertised for potential development.

The land which Samson surveyed was situated in an area known as Aston Manor. In the Domesday Book, the manor of Aston was assessed at five times the value of Birmingham and had five times the population. The Holte family had been the owners since the twelfth century, and Aston Hall remained in the family until it changed hands in the early part of the nineteenth century.

James Watt, the son of the famous engineer, whose steam engine amongst others he claimed as his own and who also befriended Edward Eastwood's cousin, the canal and railway engineer Thomas Telford, was the proud owner of Aston Hall with its fine Jacobean architecture. After the death of James Watt, Aston Hall was bought by a private company and was later opened to the public. The opening ceremony was performed by Queen Victoria in 1858, which added true credibility to this historic hall.

The life of Aston Hall and the surrounding land changed forever when Birmingham Corporation acquired the land and made use of it as a public park. Aston Hall became a museum. Much of the original parkland was inevitably sold off as building land, as by now, more and more of the surrounding farm labourers and semi-skilled workers were being drawn nearer to the industrial heartland. Soon a large workforce would be required for the growth of local industry, and new housing was necessary.

Victorian Britain was characterised by massive population growth. Between 1801 and 1901, the population of England and Wales grew from 10 million to 32.5 million. When the Princess Victoria became queen in 1837, Britain was still a rural society. When she died in 1901, the great majority of her subjects were town dwellers. The urban habitat shaped so many features of Victorian life remembered today. In fact, the Victorian age is in some respects best represented by its towns, cities, and suburbs.

In the early part of the 1850s, Aston Manor had a small population of just under seven thousand. Twenty years later, although industry and population had increased, there was still plenty of open parkland, and the area had yet to be completely transformed. In 1880 the population of Aston Manor was nearly 100,000, and the transformation from a Jacobean country house with its flowing acres of park land into the centre of intense industrial activity had begun.

Aston had woken from its deep agricultural sleep of the early centuries and had set into the industrious Victorian era. The Victorian era would be dominated by many new inventions which would change the United Kingdom and the world at large forever. None of those would have been possible without the industrialists who created new industries to satisfy the appetite of a new consumer Britain.

The Victorian period was also influenced by many famous artists, musicians, and politicians. None would ever surpass the doyen of Britishness, Winston Spencer Churchill. He was born on 30 November, 1874, the year when our very own Edward Eastwood and Edwin Samson Moore would see the birth of their Midland Vinegar Company and the foundations for that other Victorian British institution, HP Sauce.

Sir Winston Spencer Churchill (1874-1965)

The land at Aston Cross was just what Samson had been looking for. It was at the corner of Upper Thomas Street and Tower Road. There would be no transport problems, as the land overlooked the Fazeley Canal, and the newly built Aston Station meant immediate use of the Grand Junction Railway. With the by now large increase of population, Samson would have no trouble finding his eager workforce. He was equally lucky in finding the local well water hard enough to brew first-class vinegar. Samson was indeed more convinced than ever that he had all the right ingredients to start his own business. He also knew that a considerable amount of investment was needed to start his own venture.

Samson had discussed his ideas and finances with his father, Jacob. Jacob's printing business was thriving and well established, and he offered his son a loan. But although greatly appreciative, Samson had to decline the offer, telling his father that his venture would need more substantial backing. Perhaps Jacob reminded his son about the difficulty his uncle Edward Eastwood's wagon works in Chesterfield had with finance at its conception in 1863, some eleven years earlier. Possibly Jacob was the financier, being Edward's brother-in-law, or perhaps it was Jacob's father, Isaac, who provided the finances required, for he had also been in business, as a toy manufacturer.

Jacob knew that Uncle Edward's business in just over a decade had grown to such an extent that he now had a considerable fortune. Perhaps Uncle Edward was the best person to finance his new venture? With this in mind and with the forthcoming christening of his son Edwin to arrange, Samson set off for Chesterfield to pass on his good news to Uncle Edward Eastwood.

The Eastwood home, Tapton Villa, was a large, commodious residence built alongside their railway wagon business on the Brimington Road, Chesterfield. On arrival and after the good wishes and congratulations about the Moores' new birth, Samson slipped into the conversation that he would very much like his uncle to be his new-born son's godfather. Samson's son would be named Edwin Eastwood Moore. "Uncle Edward" was delighted to see his nephew was now not only an aspiring businessman like himself but also a family man.

Samson, never one to miss a business opportunity, managed to side-line "Uncle" Edward while the ladies of the house were engrossed in baby talk and prompted the subject of his pending enterprise.

Edward Eastwood had always been conscious of the financial support he had been given to start up his own railway wagon business in 1863. He also knew of Samson's other family members, who had been involved in several business enterprises throughout the nineteenth century. So, having taken to his nephew's kind offer to be his new-born son's godfather, he agreed to finance Samson's venture. Their partnership was set up.

With all the christening arrangements in hand and with Samson and his wife, Mary, having taken afternoon tea with their Uncle Edward, Aunt Abigail, and cousins, the journey home would be consumed with eager plans, ideas, and great enthusiasm for the new brewery. Samson returned to Birmingham more confident than ever of the potential success of his own enterprise, having been given the moral and financial backing he had hoped for from his uncle Edward.

Photo taken outside York Lodge on the Sutton Road, Erdington, approximately 1890-1898.

Edwin Samson Moore seated, Mary standing next to her husband (the author's great-great-grandparents), their eldest son Edwin Eastwood Moore standing with his mother. Beatrice "Minnie" Mary, the eldest child, seated in front right of Edwin. Behind "Minnie", standing, is Gertrude Alice. Seated next to her is Louisa Limer. Seated on the rug with the family dog, "Patch", is Edgar Samson. To his left, seated, is May Payne. The little girl stood at her father's lap is Dora Josephine, the youngest child. Behind her stands Edith Cecilia. Top left is Marion Ester, and standing next to her is Edgar Telford Eastwood, Edward Eastwood's son, a cousin of the Moore family. Edgar Telford Eastwood and Marian Ester Moore (the author's great-grandparents) would marry later, in 1898.

(3)

UNCLE EDWARD AND THE EASTWOODS

Edward Eastwood (1826-1910) was the uncle of Edwin Samson Moore. Edward's wife, Abigail, was the ~~brother~~ [SISTER] of Jacob Moore, Edwin Samson's father. The Eastwood Carriage & Wagon Works of Chesterfield would provide the financing for his nephew's Midland Vinegar Company.

Edward Eastwood was born on 29 January, 1826. Born during the reign of George IV (1820-1837), he was to outlive a further three heads of the monarchy: William IV (1830-1837), Victoria (1837-1901), and Edward VII (1901-1910), with Queen Victoria's reign having perhaps the most influence upon his industrious life.

Edward Eastwood and family outside Tapton Villa.

Edward was born in Hasland, Chesterfield. He was the son of a blacksmith, Joseph Eastwood, and this, the oldest of trades, was an effective apprenticeship for his future prosperity. Having learnt his trade at a very early age by his father's side, and having been in close contact with another famous native of Chesterfield, Robert Stephenson, he left Hasland as a teenager to seek his fortune in Birmingham. His first employment was as a saddler's apprentice. He also met and later married Abigail Moore, the sister of Jacob Moore, Edwin Samson Moore's father. Amongst their children was the author's great-grandfather, Edgar Telford Eastwood.

Edward Eastwood was the cousin of the canal and railway engineer Thomas Telford, and the name "Telford" has been passed down through the Eastwood and Britton families. Thomas Telford was born in Westerkirk, Eskdale, Scotland, in 1757. His father, John, died four months after his birth, leaving his mother, Janet Telford née Jackson, a widow to bring up a baby alone. She was fortunate to have a good community around her who did what they could in those early years, but it would be her brother Thomas Jackson who would be her mainstay.

Telford was helped financially throughout his early schooling by his uncle, and later in his career he found himself in the position to repay the favour and kindness given to him and his mother by the Jackson family.

Thomas Telford left school at fifteen with a good, basic education and began his apprentice as a stone mason. By 1780 he was living in Edinburgh, where his career took off. Inevitably, he moved to London, where he found himself working on Somerset House amongst other major projects. Much of Telford's life and works has been documented. Suffice it to say, he is credited with the majority of the canals, bridges, and railways we know today.

At the height of Telford's career, when he was financially secure, a cousin, James Jackson, came to him for help. James Jackson had found himself in financial difficulties. Thomas Telford paid off his debts and also paid for the apprenticeships for all of the Jackson children. He would continue to send extra money to the rest of the family.

In 1827, one of Telford's last canals to be built was the Shropshire Union Canal. One of Thomas Telford's cousins, Thomas Jackson, who by this time had completed his apprenticeship and who had also been involved in canal building, was working on the canal in Cheshire. Telford had put Thomas in charge of the cutting at Audlem. A local story tells of a time when Thomas Jackson apparently had found himself short of funds and a lady from the village had lent him £5, quite a large amount in the 1820s. In later life he would repay her kindness to him. It was said that he was responsible for having a stone erected and railings put around her grave.

Whether this was a local myth one wonders. But nevertheless, Thomas Jackson was to live most of his life in Eltham Park, Kent, and by the time of his death had become a successful and well-known contractor for canals, breakwaters, and railways throughout the country. He thought so much of Audlem and its memories for him that when he died he was interred there in the "New Cemetery" with his wife and son in 1885.

A final twist to our story was revealed during the author's research of his ancestors. Unbeknown to him at that time, the monument now found overlooking the Shropshire Union Canal in Audlem and dedicated to the Jacksons was discovered to be no more than four miles from the author's home in Nantwich, Cheshire. This quiet market town would also see one of Thomas Telford's last canal viaducts.

Thomas Telford and the Jackson family were linked in many ways, and Martha Jackson, a sister of Thomas Jackson, married Edward Eastwood's uncle, Thomas Eastwood. Thus we find via the Jacksons the cousinship of Thomas Telford and Edward Eastwood, a relationship that inspired a young Edward into the railway career from a very young age. Telford, Stephenson, and others had a huge impact on his life.

Robert Stephenson
1803-1859

son of George Stephenson
1781-1848

Thomas Telford
1757-1834

Edward moved to Birmingham at a very young age, with the connections of Telford and Stephenson having played a large part of his early life. Eager to learn, he soon left his employment at the saddler's and, aged about eighteen years, joined S. J. Claye, a soon-to-be-prosperous railway contractor from Derby.

Edward's responsibilities with this firm were considerable. His career moved forward rapidly when at the age of twenty he superintended the construction of the Erewash Valley line from Trent to Ilkeston.

It was said in later years, by those who knew him well, that Edward Eastwood was very fond of recalling a story about his early youth and career with Clayes. Edward had been promoted to the position of time-keeper for the contract from Long Eaton Old Junction to Ilkeston Junction. S. J. Claye, the main contractor, had divided his men into three gangs, each being given work under a foreman, called a "ganger".

Not long into the contract, Ganger No. 1, who was fond of the fairer sex, used to wait for the contractor to go off the site to do other duties. Then he would disappear himself for hours at a time. Ganger No. 2 knew the quality of beer in every public house in the district and would spend as much time as possible off the job sampling the "land-lord's special" in as many hostelries of the neighbourhood as he could find. Ganger No. 3 was placed under the supervision of the time-keeper, Edward Eastwood. He did the work so well, keeping his men in hand and employed in the tasks directed, that when the contractor found out the indiscretions of Gangers No. 1 and No. 2, Edward Eastwood was put in sole charge of the entire works, which he completed to the satisfaction of Mr Claye in 1847.

A typical railway "gang" of the 1840s.

John Claye, whose premises were situated on the London Road Derby, had also established himself as a large coal and ~~coak~~ [COKE] merchant. Perhaps wagons were in short supply, because in 1851 he moved to Long Eaton. Here he manufactured rolling stock. By 1861 the works employed nearly two hundred people, and ten years later up to three hundred. Edward by 1860 had become works manager. The firm expanded rapidly in the 1860s, and orders were taken from the Midland, Caleonian, North British, and Great Western Railways.

Edward Eastwood by now was an energetic and ambitious young man who was obviously intent to get on in the business world. These early experiences with railway construction and wagon building were to stand him in good stead when he later set up his own business. Edward's working life was to be dominated by the Victorian age of new industries and inventions. He himself was a true Victorian, stern, upright, god-fearing, and, most of all, a hard-working man.

Having acquired valuable experience of his profession with S. J. Claye, Edward returned to his native Chesterfield and in 1863, aged thirty-seven, set about the development of his own railway carriage and wagon works business. Edward had realised very early in his employment with S. J. Claye that the industries and commerce of the century owed much to the manufacturer of railway rolling-stock. The ready, rapid, and reliable transport of goods was vital to modern trade, and therefore the economic production of railway wagons and trucks had become one of our great national industries carried on by powerful firms in different parts of the country, with Chesterfield having long been noted as one of the competitors in this field of enterprise.

The business Edward Eastwood founded was created in the atmosphere of a great many improvements to both the machinery and the methods employed in railway wagon building. Edward's business was to benefit to the fullest extent by these advantages.

Having returned to Chesterfield, Edward began the arduous task of setting up his new venture. No enterprise can begin without sufficient financial backing to carry it through the early years of development. The author presumes Edward obtained the financial backing to set up his enterprise from his father-in-law, Isaac Moore, who was seventy-one old when Edward's business started. Isaac Moore had previously run his own thriving toy manufacturing business. Or perhaps Edward had been helped by his brother-in-law Jacob Moore, who had a thriving lithographic and printing business in Birmingham. Certainly the funds required to build his new premises would not have been achieved by Edward's own means. Even though he had reached the position of works manager at S. J. Claye, any savings would still not have allowed him sufficient funds to set up a similar enterprise from new beginnings. We should remember, however, that any financial backer would only have to conclude that Edward, as works manager and having a thorough knowledge of wagon building, could use the success of S. J. Claye's own business as an example. If he were to replicate the same in his own fashion, why should not Edward's enterprise be of equal success?

So, notwithstanding the origins of the finance required, Edward's new venture had begun. The situation of the works was eminently favourable for carrying on an industry of this kind, inasmuch as Chesterfield was in a central position and fuel, iron, and labour could be found to any extent at the cheapest rates in the industrial market. Economic production was therefore facilitated to an exceptional extent, and the skilful arrangement and organisation of the works, together with the liberality with which improved machinery had been utilised, brought these workshops to a high standard of efficiency. Science and favourable circumstances had contributed to this end, and Edward Eastwood's productions were soon to be found on every line in the country.

The works were situated along the Midland Railway line, about a quarter of a mile from the Chesterfield station. They comprised a long, shed-like structure, with a frontage of 450 feet to the high road, and the iron and timber yards at the rear of the building. At each end of the building was a gateway entrance. The commodious offices were situated over the entrance at the Chesterfield end. The interior of the factory was arranged into erecting, fitting, moulding, and wood-working shops. A convenient office on the ground floor commanded a good view down the centre of the factory, which gave supervision over every department.

Internal view of the Eastwood Carriage and Wagon Works circa 1895.

The factory contained powerful machinery of the most improved types. Labour-saving appliances and machine tools, both for wood-working and iron-working, were in constant operation. All the parts were made on the premises, and in the wheel-making shops and smithies, planting, turning, moulding and fitting out were done in a very business-like manner. Steam power was supplied by a compact engine, and the whole arrangement was designed so as to facilitate rapid output with effective supervision.

Great stores of sound, well-seasoned timber were always on hand, and every facility was provided for the prompt execution of heavy emergent orders. There were over a hundred mechanics employed, and with powerful machinery in use, the heaviest orders could be dealt with without interfering with the ordinary arrangements. The business was a very extensive one, wagons and trucks being supplied for all descriptions of railway transport and for all parts of the country.

The business kept to the highest of standards by constantly moving with the times and introducing improvements. As the natural advantages of the position could not be rivalled, the Eastwood's works maintained a leading position in this important industry. The prosperity of modern Chesterfield and its position as an industrial centre at the turn of the twentieth century owed much to Edward Eastwood's enterprise, and these busy workshops formed one of the representative industrial seats of the district.

Having established his railway carriage and wagons business, Edward saw the need for repair workshops across the county. For in a colliery district the subject of railway wagons, their price, their construction, and above all, the repairs which were necessary to keep them efficient were a perennial and a burning question.

Many of the difficulties which the mine owners had to face were of their own making, insofar as they had been foolish enough to purchase rolling stock at rates at which it would be absolutely impossible to turn out reliable work, the result being a series of bills for repair which caused them to quickly come to the conclusion that the Eastwood wagon would make more economical sense. Edward Eastwood's business as a maker and repairer of railway wagons held a tradition that demanded good work with good materials. That not every firm was governed by such high motives was well shown by an interesting museum at the works which contained numerous examples of bad and even disgraceful work removed from wagons sent for repairs.

One of the chief ways in which the business proved a boon to the wagon user was when Edward's business undertook the whole duty of keeping the trucks in repair, working either by contract or by the piece, according to circumstances. The colliery owner or manufacturer was saved the endless worry of maintaining his own wagon-repairing plant. He further avoided the expense of having the damaged truck hauled into its own sidings from the point at which the breakdown occurred. In order that his business could be carried through with a minimum of delay, Edward established depots at Ambergate, Nottingham, Peterborough, Stavely, Blackwell, Morton, and Toton sidings, besides several other places.

All these were highly convenient as wagon-repairing centres for the reason that wherever the truck was, there was always a good train on the way to one or other of them to which it could be attached. Edward Eastwood's business continued to flourish, and by the 1880s a local business directory in Sandiacre listed him as a railway wagon builder. So with his main business premises at Chesterfield and now Sandiacre, and with his coverage of localised depots, Edward had established a large concern.

He further assisted the man of commerce by building wagons which could be relied upon to endure the heavy strains to which they were inevitably to be subjected. Practically the whole of the work was done on his premises, only a few special forgoings having to be ordered from elsewhere.

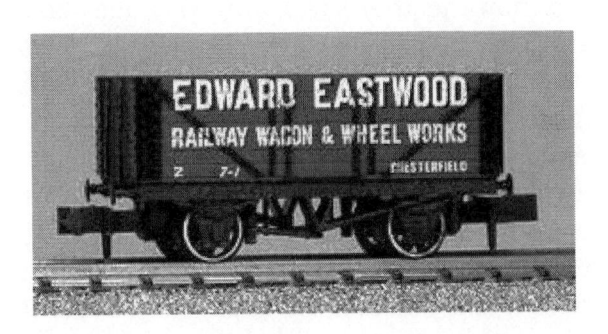

Throughout the main works, which occupied five acres, adjoining the Midland Railway at Chesterfield there was an indefinable air of efficiency. The great logs of oak coming from Danzig or Strettin in Prussia were cut into lengths by great circular saws, planed, bored, and given the finishing touches with a speed which speaks eloquently of disciplined industry.

In the machine shops, the ponderous steam hammers and shearing, punching, and drilling machines dealt with the metal parts with equal rapidity. The erecting shop was capable of holding forty wagons at a time, and here the completed parts were assembled into a finished structure.

This then was the principal business that Edward had established, although he later had many other industrial concerns in the Midlands and the country at large. He became a director of Broad Oaks Iron Foundry, later to be known as C. P. Markham's, which in recent history was responsible for manufacturing the cutting turbine circular saws that made the Channel Tunnel possible. He was also a director of Singer & Co., one of the first car manufacturers, and, as we later learn, a financer of and partner in the Midland Vinegar Company.

Edward Eastwood's family home was built alongside his business premises in 1863. It had long been the fashion of many well-to-do industrialists of the Victorian period to make their homes in houses alongside their place of work, sometimes remaining there well into old age. Edward, who had known Robert Stephenson's home at Tapton House, emulated one of his heroes by naming his own home in Tapton "Tapton Villa". Although not in the same style or structure as Stephenson's, it was nonetheless an imposing home for this nineteenth-century Chesterfield industrialist.

Tapton Villa would remain as the family home for three-quarters of a century. In 1938 it was demolished to make way for office expansion and new wagon repair shops. The house, however, had been used as additional office space as early as 1910, and the atmosphere of the house alongside the railway works was best described by Mary Hooton, Edward Eastwood's granddaughter, who had worked there all those years ago.

"Something of the past always seemed to linger about the long room which had been the family living and dining room. The black marbled fireplace, the large gilt framed mirror above, still in position, and a heavy white marble clock, ticking away as it must have done over many decades. I remember the Wagon Works, the old Victorian crane in the yard was still working when I joined the staff in 1929. All the clerk's desks were tall Dickensian type design, even that of the owner's son George Albert Eastwood, in his office which was situated near the house. He always stood at it to work and sign letters. I never saw him use the tall stools that were there, not even in old age."

Edward Eastwood (1826-1910)

Beneath the offices was the original coach house for the family. My mother, Ada Moore Eastwood, remembered the carriage and "dog cart" for the ladies of the house.

The garden had been much reduced and neglected over the years. The conservatory, of which Edward Eastwood was very proud, was long since gone. My mother remembered, when on a visit, hearing that Edward had once sat up all night to watch a choice, rare plant open for a brief moment. His collection of orchids had become a hobby and was much admired by fellow enthusiasts. Mother often spoke of visits to Tapton Villa. She described Grandmother Abigail, steel knitting needles in hand, busy with socks for her sons, small and birdlike, but the dominant personality of the house. Mother remembered the family prayers, the maids joining the family, one or other of the sons hurrying back to be on time, and Grandfather looking over his glasses with mounting disapproval.

Photo taken outside Tapton Villa. Seated centre, Edward Eastwood and Abigail Eastwood (née Moore), the author's great-great-grandparents. Seated on the left, Josephine, seated right, Blanche, and standing at the back of the group is the author's great-grandfather, Edgar Telford Eastwood.

Tapton Villa was home to Edward and Abigail Eastwood and to their large family of eight children, which was a typical size for the Victorians. Of their five sons and three daughters, the eldest was Edward Isaac. Born in 1851, he had no desire to join his father in the family wagon business. Instead, he took a career in engineering. Unfortunately his life was cut short. While employed on business in St Petersburg, Russia, he died of pneumonia. Although only in his early thirties, he had a problem with alcohol periodically, having bouts of drinking even though his father had offered him £500 if he could refrain for six months. £500 in the 1880s was a considerable amount of money. Unfortunately he died and was buried in the Smolensky Cemetery, a young man of only thirty-three years. Tragedy had fallen on the Eastwood family twenty years earlier when their second-eldest son, Joseph, born 1852, died aged fourteen just three years after Edward had opened his wagon works. It was said he fell into a vat of boiling water and drowned.

The Eastwood brothers: Edgar Telford, George Albert, Thomas Moore, Edward Isaac.

George Albert was the third-eldest son. Born 1860, he would play a large part in the Eastwood wagon works beside his father and later take over the firm after his father's death in 1910. Edward and Abigail's other children were Mary, who married into the Oliver family that owned the Broad Oaks Iron Works in Chesterfield. Edward Eastwood was the chairman of this company, which was later bought out by the Markham family, well-known nineteenth — and twentieth-century industrialists who were also prominent in a 1940s sex scandal and murder in Nairobi, Kenya. A film,

White Mischief, took up the story of these wealthy English upper-class aristocrats and their hedonistic behaviour. Markham's designed the huge cutting & boring wheels that cut the Channel Tunnel in 1987.

The other children of Edward and Abigail, Ada Moore Eastwood, Josephine, and Thomas, took no active interest in the family business or other concerns. Edward and Abigail's fourth son was the author's great-grandfather, Edgar Telford Eastwood, who was born in 1862. Edgar was named "Telford" after the railway and canal engineer Thomas Telford, who was a cousin of Edward Eastwood. Edgar at the 1891 census was described as the assistant superintendent of the Eastwood Railway Wagon Works. In his late twenties he would go and live at the home of his cousin Edwin Samson Moore at York Lodge Erdington. Samson Moore employed him at the family's Midland Vinegar Company.

There are no records of why he left the wagon works, but it should be noted that by 1891 his brother George Albert, who was two years older than him, was described in the same 1891 census as the superintendent of the railway wagon works. Perhaps the brothers didn't get along. Whether there was a family argument about the way forward for the business or just sibling rivalry, Edward Eastwood must have called upon his nephew Samson Moore to help. It should be remembered that at that time Edgar was twenty-nine and still single. With no apparent ties to Chesterfield, he probably thought that a fresh start away from the wagon works would act as a new beginning. Edward may have thought this an opportunity for his son to work alongside the Moores and keep an eye on the Eastwood's investment. It was during his stay with them, that he met and fell in love with his much younger cousin Marion Esther Moore. A relationship was struck up, and family rumour has it that Marion became pregnant and they quickly married. Such relationships, although legal, were normally forbidden in Victorian times. The couple married amidst family scorn, which only added to the rumours.

With an allowance from both parents and a salary position at the brewery, Edgar and Marion set up home further up the Sutton Road from the Moores. Later living alongside them were the author's grandfather and his family, the Brittons. William Stanley Britton met Edgar and Marion Eastwood's daughter Vera Josephine over a game of tennis on the Britton's tennis courts at the rear of their home, Melrose House on the Sutton Road. Their relationship blossomed, and they fell in love and married.

These, then, are the ancestors of Edward and Abigail Eastwood. Edward and his business are so much the architects of our story, for without its success his cousin Edwin Samson Moore would never have had the funds available to begin the Midland Vinegar Company.

The size of the Eastwood empire cannot be underestimated. The wagon works would have been of equal value and capacity in production to, say, a modern-day car factory, turning out tens of thousands of railway wagons, which were bought by every industry to transport goods throughout the country and the world at large. With thousands of wagons coming off the production lines, the Eastwoods were at the forefront of those decades known as "railway mania".

Edward Eastwood died in 1910. In his will he left in 2013 values the astonishing amount of 45.5 million pounds. So much was his business a success that when he died in 1910 his philanthropic activities in Chesterfield were acknowledged in his obituary, which was taken up in the *Derbyshire Times* of Saturday, 11 June, 1910.

"Chesterfield has lost one of her best friends by the death of Alderman Edward Eastwood. A man of many parts, he will stand out chiefly as one who during his lifetime essayed to use his wealth for the benefit of the town of his adoption and the relief of the suffering of those amongst who he lived."

Edward's business life and ramifications were very large. Apart from his carriage and wagon works, already previously discussed, he was also involved with a great many industrious projects of the time. He was a chief shareholder and director of the Midland Vinegar Company, makers of HP Sauce. His wide interests included lace industry and lace machinery manufacturer, at Long Eaton, and also a large shipping concern, the Horsley Line of West Hartlepool. In recognition of his interest with that firm, one of their first new boats was named *Eastwood*. The boat was built by W. Gray & Co. for George Horsley & Son and was launched on 29 August, 1904.

Edward Eastwood always took an active part in public life. He was for many years a member of the Chesterfield Board of Guardians of the old Chesterfield and Tapton Burial Board. He was a member and for several years chairman of the Brimington School Board and also a member of the Chesterfield School Board from 1886 until 1895. His interests with education lasted up to the time of his death. One of his latest acts was to make certain concessions to the county council in connection with the New High School for Girls in Chesterfield and also grant free rent for the use of a field in Infirmary Road for playing purposes. In 1885, Edward Eastwood was placed on the Commission of the Peace for the Borough of Chesterfield, and ten years later on that of the county of Derby.

Edward Eastwood will be best remembered for his numerous and generous benefactions to the town of Chesterfield, especially in connection with the Chesterfield and North Derbyshire Hospital. From an early day he had taken a great interest in this institution, an interest which grew with his increasing years. But it was in 1900 it assumed large proportions. For some years prior to this, a new medical wing to the hospital had been greatly needed, and much pressure had been brought to the board of management to provide the same, but without success. Edward Eastwood stepped into the breach and offered to provide a building capable of containing twenty beds if the board would accept control of the same. The first intimation of Edward's intention was given in the following letter addressed to Dr George Booth, chairman of the Chesterfield school board, and dated 9 January, 1900.

"Dear Sir, I understand the Board is willing to sell the Durrant Road School and offices as they stand for the sum of £2500. This being so I am prepared to purchase the same for the purpose of adopting it as a medical ward to be attached to the North Derbyshire Hospital and Dispensary adjoining subject to the Board of that institution accepting it. And I am willing to supplement this gift with £1000 towards the necessary structural alterations and the furnishing. Your assistance in the carrying out of this scheme will be much appreciated by yours truly, Edward Eastwood"

The offer was gratefully accepted, and in 1901 Edward Eastwood was put in possession of the Durrant Road Schools. At once set he about to have the building converted for the purpose required. The buildings were enlarged, fitted and furnished as medical wards, and connected with the main hospital buildings by means of a covered way. This gift must have represented more than £4000. The buildings were opened on 9 April, 1902, with a befitting ceremony by Earl Manvers.

The day before, Chesterfield Corporation met and unanimously decided to add Alderman Eastwood's name to the ancient roll of freeman of the borough, which dates back to 1644 and whose most recent addition was that of Lord Roberts. In the course of his opening speech, Earl Manvers paid a fitting tribute to Edward Eastwood, saying his name would go down to future generations as a very great benefactor of Chesterfield. Earl Manvers laid due stress on the indebtedness of the whole district to Edward Eastwood, and although Ald. Eastwood was the last one to desire any recognition other than a generous support on behalf of the public to the new institution, the corporation voiced the feelings of the town by according to the donor the highest honour they had in their power to bestow, the Freedom of the Borough.

Edward Eastwood purchased Holywell House and the land that formed part of Brewery Meadow ostensibly for the purpose of preventing the hospital being built in. Subsequently he gave part of the Brewery Meadow as a site for the Nurses' Home.

Even this did not exhaust his generosity, for in connection with the extension of the hospital, Edward Eastwood and the members of his family were again found amongst the largest contributors. Mrs Eastwood gave £1000 to the hospital shortly before her death. This was the largest gift up to that time, and it was suitably acknowledged by a marble tablet erected in the male ward, which bears the following inscription.

"The Governors of this hospital have erected this tablet to commemorate the gift of £1000 by Mrs Edward Eastwood, of Tapton, Chesterfield, and to express their high appreciation of her great generosity and kindness to the sufferers of this institution. 7 Sept. 1903"

Edward Eastwood was appointed on the board of management of the hospital on 14 March, 1883, and on 11 March, 1891, he was elected a vice-president, which position he held up to the time of his death.

In 1908 Edward Eastwood further added to his public benefactions by the erection of eight alms houses for gentlewomen in the Infirmary Road, in close contiguity to the land on which by his generosity the Nurses' Home in connection with the Chesterfield Hospital had been erected.

The purpose Edward Eastwood had in view was described in the *Derbyshire Times* of that time.

"Eventide." A more appropriate name could not have been given to the beautiful homes for aged gentlewomen which with his well-known philanthropy, Edward Eastwood has just erected in Chesterfield. Here in comfort and amid beautiful surroundings, eight ladies will in future be able to spend the eventide of their life under conditions which do not rob them of their self-respect or independence. The occupants of the houses by the terms of the bequest must have a small income which will enable them to furnish the little houses and keep themselves in the necessaries of life. This is all, but it is just that practical touch which gives point to Mr Eastwood's true philanthropic intentions. He desires to assist without pauperism; he wishes his gift to be such as any lady can accept without loss of that becoming pride which often makes the really needy of this class suffer silently where those of less tender feelings flourish on public charity. It is superfluous for us to say how much the benefaction is appreciated in Chesterfield, where Mr Eastwood will ever be regarded as one of the best and worthiest of our citizens. May this eventide be as serene and bright as he has endeavoured to ensure that of others now and in the future shall be.

Edward Eastwood took an active part in the formation of the Chesterfield and Derbyshire Institute of Engineers in 1870 and was appointed treasurer, a position which he held until 1905, when he resigned due to his advancing years. He was elected a life member in recognition of his services. The institution soon changed name to that of the Chesterfield and Midland Counties and was later known as the Midlands Counties Institute. It will be remembered as the institution which initiated the scheme to perpetuate the memory of George Stephenson in the town. Edward Eastwood was most active in furthering this scheme and bringing the Soiree to a successful issue. The Memorial Hall for some time was held by trustees but is now a public library.

In politics, Edward Eastwood was an ardent Liberal. He was at the time of his death the president of the Chesterfield Division Liberal Association, a position he had held for many years. It was to be the highlight of his son, George Albert Eastwood's, life when that exponent of Liberalism, Mr Lloyd George, visited Chesterfield in July 1924 and stayed at Brambling House as a guest.

Edward Eastwood died in 1910 a very wealthy man. He left a will of over a half of a million pounds. The bulk of this was left to his son George Albert, who had worked devotedly in the wagon works was its sole inheritor. He had no wish to remain in Tapton Villa and by 1911 had purchased and moved into Brambling House, a large Victorian house in spacious grounds on the outskirts of Chesterfield. Its ivy-clad walls were a notable landmark visible at many points in the town.

George Albert Eastwood, like his father, would play a large part in Chesterfield life. He was a justice of the peace, an alderman, and three times mayor of Chesterfield. He was on the board of many local institutions. Apart from being the proprietor of the family business, he was also chairman of J. & W. Wells colliery proprietors, a director of several other Derbyshire collieries and concerns, a director of Singer and Co., the famous motor cycle and car manufacturers, and The Midland Finance Company.

George Albert Eastwood (1860-1934).

George Albert Eastwood, like his father, was a very generous man, and his benefactions to the people of Chesterfield are described in the following pages. The Eastwoods took great interest with the education of Chesterfield citizens. With this in mind, George Albert secured the education of future generations with the purchase of land adjoining the houses known as "Eventide", previously built by his father, Edward.

On the land George Albert purchased in the early 1920s was built the Chesterfield Technical College. He also donated the sum of £25,000 for the building of the college. A stone was laid on 22 October, 1924, to commemorate the erection of the first section of the building and also the land which George Albert gave. Over the years more extensions have been added, giving the students of Chesterfield much-needed space for their studies.

Many other generous gifts were made by George Albert over the years, including Holywell House, the grey stone building that adjoined the hospital precinct. This was donated as premises for the Nurses' Home. The many contributions of the Eastwood family on the hill prompted someone to speak of it as "The Hill of the Good Samaritan".

Although George Albert Eastwood's benefactions were many, perhaps none surpassed his gift of Hasland House. With its fifteen acres of grounds, this magnificent property was purchased by George Albert to perpetuate the memory of his father, Edward Eastwood.

Hasland House has a history which is lost in the past. The following extracts from the *Derbyshire Courier* of Saturday, 5 July, 1913, try to unearth some of the history of Hasland House.

It is not known who built Hasland House or who built the original portion. It has been added to on a number of occasions. It is a delightful old building, three-storied, surrounded by some fine old trees, and with a nice, old-fashioned flower and kitchen garden. Then there is a tennis lawn, which was made by the last occupier, Mr Eric D. Swanwick, and the two fields together extend to about 15 acres. The smaller of the two has been used of late years as the cricket ground of Hasland Church Institute Cricket Club.

The first owner of Hasland House who is remembered by the Chesterfield residents of today, was the late Mr Josiah Claughton who, in the middle of the last century, was an eminent wholesale chemist in Chesterfield. His business premises were on Low Pavement, on the west side of the entrance to the Old Three Tuns Inn, but the business died out with the demise of Mr Claughton himself. He left a son, Mr Willis Claughton, who was well known as a wine and spirit merchant, and the business with which he was concerned is now carried on under the name of Messrs J. B. White and Sons, High Street, Chesterfield.

Another son, who died in early life, used to reside in Station Road in the premises which are now used as a printing works. Hasland House, however, was not built by Mr Josiah Claughton. The first part of it is probably 150 years old, and almost entirely made of brick.

Hasland House circa 1913. The house and grounds of fifteen acres was given over to the people of Chesterfield and officially opened to the public on 2 July, 1913. From that time it was known as "Eastwood Park".

*Hasland House 1913.
C. P. Markham's magnificent fountain from Ringwood Hall in the foreground.*

The *Derbyshire Courier* of Saturday, 13 July, 1913, continues with the history of Hasland House.

The Claughton family, in the Chesterfield mind, was closely associated with Hasland House, as it was occupied for many years by four of Mr Claughtons daughters, and there are people today who were in the service of those ladies when in residence. In addition to his two sons, Mr Claughton had six daughters. One of them became a Mrs Clay, and she married a second time and became the wife of Mr William Drabble, solicitor of Chesterfield. By her first husband (Mr Clay) she had an only daughter, who became the wife of Mr Bright, a gentleman from the district, and the misses Bright, of the close, Hasland, are daughters of the marriage and therefore, granddaughters of Mr Josiah Claughton. This lady was the wife of Mr Beedham, a solicitor. One son of the latter followed in his father's footsteps and became a solicitor; whilst another, the Rev. Maurice Beedham, took holy orders, and became rector of Bridgnorth, Salop. For many years the other four daughters of Josiah Claughton resided together at Hasland House: but one by one they passed away until the holding became the sole property of Miss Catherine Claughton, who died in the year 1895. By her will she bequeathed the house to her nephew, the Rev. Maurice Beedham, rector of Bridgnorth.

Shortly after this time the Rev. Maurice Beedham resigned his living and came to reside at Hasland House. Many older residents doubtless remember the sturdy figure of the revered Gentleman as he moved about the village, for he soon became well known in the place. He, however, did not live very long to enjoy his inheritance and he left a widow and one son. Mrs Beedham continued to reside at Hasland House, but it was not very long before she too, passed away, and the property passed to her only son, John Arthur Beedham, who had been engaged in the dominion for a good many years. Upon the death of his mother, Mr John A. Beedham came over to England, but as his interests were more in Canada than in the old country, he decided to dispose of the property. It was put up for auction in 1904, and the purchaser was the late Mr Bernard Lucas. It is from the trustees of Mr Lucas that George Albert Eastwood purchased the Park.

In making his gift known to the Town Council, George Albert wrote to the Town clerk in 1912 stating that he desired to place no restrictions upon the Corporation in their control or the management of the property, except that it should be kept as a park or public recreation ground under the Public Health Acts, exactly like the Queens Parks for the inhabitants of the borough for ever.

Besides containing a house which for some time was the residence of Mr Eric Swanwick, and which will, besides housing the caretaker, serve as a branch reading room and library, the grounds possess a large conservatory, a magnificent fountain, which was the gift of Ald. C. P. Markham, and a wealth of old trees and any amount of grass areas. The park is shut off from the main road by a handsome stone wall and wrought-iron railing, in the *centre of which are the entrance gates bearing the borough arms and the words "Eastwood Park".*

For the people of Chesterfield and Hasland in particular, perhaps nothing more than Eastwood Park can represent the gift to the local inhabitants made by George Albert Eastwood in memory of his father, Edward. Of course this monument should also be thought of as the very essence of a tribute to the skilled workforce of the Eastwood wagon works who, it could be said, were equally responsible for the success of that company. In 2012 the local authority, through various secured grants, are transforming the park and spending a million pounds to bring it into the twenty-first century. However, if we turn the clock back to 1913, then the following accolade could not be more appropriate to Edward Eastwood as described on the opening of Eastwood Park.

2 July, 1913, was a memorable day for George Albert Eastwood, for prior to the opening of Eastwood Park, there had been a special meeting of the town council at the Stephenson Memorial Hall. This was to confer on Alderman Eastwood the Freedom of the Borough. The proceedings were initiated by the Town Clerk reading the following motion.

That this council hereby, in pursuance of the Honorary Freedom of Borough Act, 1885, confer upon Alderman George Albert Eastwood, J. P., the Honorary Freedom of the Borough of Chesterfield, in recognition of the eminent public services rendered by him to the Borough, as manifested not only in the performance of his varied duties as a member of the Town Council and of other Public Bodies and in the active personal work and generous support which he has given to the Chesterfield and North Derbyshire Hospital as a member and, for some years, as Vice-Chairman of the Board of Management, but especially in his thoughtful and magnificent gift to the town of Hasland House and the adjoining (to be known in future as Eastwood Park) for the free use of the public for ever. That the Town Council accordingly hereby admits the said George Albert Eastwood to be an Honorary Freeman of the Borough of Chesterfield.

George Albert was the first son of a freeman to be made a freeman. After the proceedings had taken place, a civic procession was formed. The route from the council offices to the new park was lined by crowds of people, in spite of the fact that the distance was nearly two miles. On arrival at Hasland, there was displayed large numbers of flags, bunting, festoons, etc. The mayor handed a gold souvenir key to Miss Eastwood (Susie Blanche Eastwood, George Albert's niece and the daughter of his elder brother Edward Isaac, who had died in Russia at the early age of thirty-three). The key was not only a souvenir but also the key to unlock the main entrance gates.

"It gives me great pleasure," the mayor said, "to present to you this key to open the park which your uncle has so generously given to the borough."

Miss Eastwood unlocked the gates and on entering the park received a bouquet of carnations, roses, and lilies-of-the-valley, from Mrs Dorothy Knight. Miss Eastwood was loudly cheered and said how very much she appreciated the honour of being asked to perform that little ceremony. She thanked the corporation for the gift of so magnificent a key, which she would always treasure as a memento of the occasion.

The procession then continued along the driveway to an improvised platform, which was emblazed with plants and flowers from the conservatory. After the presentation of a casket to George Albert, his subsequent vote of thanks, and other speeches, the invited guests had tea in a large marquee at the invitation of Ald. Eastwood.

HP Sauce My Ancestors' Legacy

The civic dignitaries leading the procession into Eastwood Park: L. R. Mace (bearer), Mr Paul Bradley, Chief Constable Mr R. Kilpatrick, Miss Blanche Eastwood, The Mayor, Major W.B. Robinson, Borough Justice of the Peace, Mr George A. Booth, Alderman Mr Charles Paxton Markham.

George Albert Eastwood (standing centre stage) during his inauguration at the opening of Eastwood Park.

Photo taken from the stage facing the huge crowds in Eastwood Park, all in their Sunday best.

From the Derbyshire Times, Saturday, 5 July, 1913, an artist's impression of George Albert Eastwood standing next to the casket presented to him from the people of Hasland in recognition of his gift of Eastwood Park. Hasland House stands in the background.

HP Sauce My Ancestors' Legacy

Adjoining Hasland House a public hall was built. This was made possible as a gift by Mr B. C. Lucas of Clifton. At the time Eastwood Park was opened in 1913, Hasland House was attached to stables. It was on this site that the new public hall was built and opened on 22 July, 1914. The magnificent fountain donated by Ald. C. P. Markham stands in the foreground.

The photograph below was taken in 1988. The original Hasland House given with the park by George Albert Eastwood is long since gone, and a more modest property now replaces it. A flower bed is all that remains of the once-splendid fountain originally donated by Ald. C. P. Markham in 1913. Where's the fountain?

The fountain that now adorns Eastwood Park has had an eventful life, with several homes. In 1913 George Albert Eastwood gave Hasland House and its fifteen acres of land to the people of Chesterfield and Hasland. We first learn of the fountain in 1913, when it was donated to Eastwood Park by Alderman C. P. Markham, who at that time was deputy mayor. During the thanks given by George Albert Eastwood on the opening day he said, "I cannot imagine what Alderman Markham was thinking about to let such a magnificent fountain come away from "Ringwood". It was past explanation; it was a fountain that would do credit to any park or any place in England."

Ringwood Hall can boast to being connected for over a hundred years with the remarkable story of the Staveley Works and the lives of the industrialists who made Ringwood their home. *Burke's Peerage* of 1809 records George Hodgkinson Barrow at the Hall, and *Bagshaw's Gazetteer* of 1846 mentions the Hall as "not long built".

A gardening journal of 1876 names Barrow as "the builder of the Hall about fifty years ago". In 1840 George Hodgkinson Barrow asked his wealthy young brother

Richard to take over the loss-making coal and iron works. Richard not only expanded them but also built the village of Barrow Hill, complete with school, church, and workman's institute for employees.

Richard Barrow lived at Ringwood Hall until his death in 1865. The *Derbyshire Times* of 18 January, 1865, records some five thousand people lining his funeral procession route from Ringwood Hall to Staveley Churchyard, where he was buried in the same tomb as his brother George.

Only one year earlier he had formed the Staveley Coal and Iron Company and invited his friend Charles Markham to leave his job in the Midland Railway in Derby and be the managing director. Charles accepted, and the Markhams came to Staveley.

The Barrow family continued to live at Ringwood after Richard's death, but in *Kelly's Trade Directory 1895* the "Marquis Piedilermini de Saliceto" is listed as living there. Local people said he was an Italian nobleman. Charles Markham died in 1888 and was succeeded by his son Charles Paxton Markham, who went on to make the Staveley Company one of the biggest concerns in the country.

In 1907 Charles Paxton Markham bought Ringwood Hall and made it his home. He was a very generous man and believed in a good day's pay for a good day's work. On Sunday afternoons he would open the grounds at Ringwood so that his workmen and families could have a day out and enjoy themselves.

A mayor of Chesterfield three times, he gave Tapton House and grounds, his former family home, to the Borough of Chesterfield to be used as a school. Tapton House was purchased from its previous owner, George Stephenson. After Charles Markham died in 1926, Ringwood was given to the Staveley Company to be used for the benefit of employees.

Local stories about the hall say that Captain Webb stayed there and swam in Ringwood Lake. Local people working at the hall and in the gardens have seen the ghost of a lady dressed in Victorian attire and think it could be the former Mrs Lowe, the wife of George Hodgkinson.

Ringwood Hall circa 1900

Ringwood Hall was the home of the Markham family. Charles Markham married Rosa Paxton in 1862. Her father, Sir Joseph Paxton, was the designer of the Crystal Palace where the great exhibition of 1851 was held in Hyde Park.

For about seventy years the fountain remained at Eastwood Park, where it had been originally intended by C. P. Markham. In the early 1980s, the Chesterfield Council and powers that be decide to relocate the fountain into New Square Chesterfield and, for reasons better known to themselves, to rename it the "Peace Fountain".

One can only presume that common sense prevailed. With the recent new funding available, up to one million pounds, to regenerate Eastwood Park, it was thought the fountain should be returned to its rightful home. Today it stands proud in Eastwood Park, as seen in the photo above.

Eastwood Park, a century after its first conception as a place for families to relax, as desired by George Albert Eastwood in memory of his father, Edward Eastwood. Charles Paxton Markham would have also been pleased to see his magnificent gift of a fountain reinstated where he had originally intended it to be. Mr Charles Paxton Markham's gift to Eastwood Park and his generosity to Hasland and Chesterfield were typical of many Victorian industrialists, and their acts of philanthropy were much appreciated.

The Markham family can trace their ancestors back to 1066 and Roger de Busali from Normandy. In 1989 the author contacted Sir Charles Markham (1924-2006) who at that time was the chairman of the infamous Muthaiga Club in Nairobi. He was forthcoming with his family history, which should give the reader some idea about what happened to the family ancestral homes, Tapton House and Ringwood Hall, both of which were left to the public. The following letter is in reply to the author's letter of introduction to him.

28th March 1989

Dear Mr Britton,

Thank you for your letter of the 7th March which Muthaiga Club forwarded to me.

Yes, all my family came from Chesterfield and the Charles Paxton Markham was my great-uncle. It was his father who built up Staveley Iron Coal and Steel and the firm called Markham & Co still exists near the railway station, although now it has nothing to do with the family and is part of Staveley.

The story of Tapton is interesting. It was indeed the family home which C. P. Markham inherited on the death of his father. I don't know the exact date but there was a real family row when Charles Paxton Markham got involved in a messy divorce case in the early twenties and none of his family would talk to him or even allow him in their homes. This resulted, incidentally, in my father being disinherited as he was meant to be the heir to the very considerable fortune Markham made. He died with no children in 1926.

Tapton should have been left to my father, but in his rage Markham one morning decided he did not want the place and rather than let my father have it he gave the place, plus all the considerable quantity of land to the Chesterfield City Council, all free of charge. He then moved to Ringwood Hall at Chesterfield. Tapton House, once owned by the famous George Stephenson from whom it was purchased by my great-grandfather, is now a school, I think, and some of the land there is also a golf course.

The only family interest left at Tapton is the private Markham family burial ground, and the Corporation are meant to maintain it in view of the gift made to them. A notable exception who is neither buried there nor mentioned on the wall of Markhams who were not buried there is that of C. P. Markham! It was all rather tragic and from what I can gather

C. P. left his wife and went off with a young girl who was not only his ward but some twenty-five years his junior, so you can well imagine there was quite a scandal at the time. She of course became a very rich woman indeed and I do know she re-married and had a son, but I have forgotten her new name. Way back in the early fifties and the Emergency in Kenya I met an officer at Muthaiga and he told me his mother had been married to a Markham, but he said he did not know the details, except that she was his second wife. As he mentioned Chesterfield, that Markham must have been the C. P. one.

I am sorry I have no photographs. My only visits to Tapton are to attend funerals and I have not been inside the very large house. I always thought it somewhat ugly from the outside. I often wonder what my future might have been had there not been that family break-up over divorce.

Yours Sincerely,
Charles Markham

Tapton House circa 1900. Charles Markham, in his letter to the author of 1989, thought it "somewhat ugly from the outside".

The Markham family were witness to another well-known scandal, this time in Kenya during the 1940s. Charles Markham in 1989 recalled an incident which took place at the Muthaiga Club in Nairobi between his father and Lord Erroll, the debonair twenty-second Earl of Erroll, Hereditary Lord High Constable of Scotland and one of the greatest womanisers of Kenya's notorious "Happy Valley" set. Charles Markham (1899-1952) stood at the men's bar of the Muthaiga Club one morning in September 1940. He was having a drink with Lord Errol. Charles Markham, the wealthy British colliery owner, had been lured to Kenya by his passion for hunting big game. The Muthaiga Country Club in Nairobi, which had opened in 1913 and was a symbol of the colonial settlers' power, had become a magnet for those seeking a gentleman's club, with all the privileges that came with it, deep in the heart of Africa.

There was nothing unusual about that warm morning of September 1940 until Charles Markham turned to Lord Erroll and said, "You know, Erroll, if you went home and served in the army for two or three years, you could come back and become the leader of the European settlers."

Looking Markham straight in the eyes and with a slightly mocking smile on his lips, Erroll replied: "I'd rather f . . . than fight."

Markham was appalled. He threw his glass of whisky in Erroll's face and strode out of the bar with the laughter of his companion ringing in his ears. Although his actions were inspired by sentiments which the overwhelming majority of the members undoubtedly supported, it was Markham who had to resign from the club. Erroll was a member of the committee.

Just four months later, on 24 January, 1941, Captain the Hon. Josslyn Victor Hay, Twenty-Second Earl of Erroll, Hereditary Lord High Constable of Scotland, disappeared while driving home in a hired Buick from a dinner in nearby Karen. His body was later found in the rear of the vehicle at a crossroads on the Ngong-Nairobi road, just a few miles from Nairobi. He had been shot in the head.

Local suspicion claimed he had been having an affair with Diana, the wife of Sir Delves Broughton. Broughton was tried for murder but acquitted. The case remains unsolved to this day and sparked a frenzy of rumours and speculation that brought about a film in 1988, *White Mischief*, which only added to the mystique of this exclusive society.

Charles Markham's father [Son], the wealthy collier and industrialist Charles Paxton Markham (whose mother, Rosa Paxton, was the daughter of Sir Joseph Paxton, who in 1851 designed the Crystal Palace in Hyde Park for the Great Exhibition) would find the expansion of his empire in the late 1880s more an act of good fortune and timing than brilliant business acumen. The fate of Markham & Co. Limited in the twentieth century perhaps owed a great deal of its success to Edward Eastwood, as we will now discover.

Edward Eastwood and his wife, Abigail Moore's, son George Albert had a twin sister, Louise Mary. Louise would marry a John Oliver., but the Eastwood association with this family would begin with John Oliver's grandfather, also called John, born at the beginning of the eighteenth century.

John Oliver, like Edward Eastwood, had begun his career as a blacksmith. He was also a friend of the great railway engineer George Stephenson. John had a son called William who was born in 1828. He joined his father in his smithy at a very early age, and between them they developed the business of blacksmithing, coach building, and wheelwright work. Their business soon employed up to forty tradesmen. In 1854 they moved to larger premises, which would be known as the Victoria Ironworks Foundry.

John Oliver died in 1862, and William carried on the family business. William's son John married Edward Eastwood's daughter Mary Louise. The foundry business of William expanded, and they were soon manufacturing pump engines, pit tub wheels, and associated products for most of the collieries in the district and further afield.

By 1865 William formed a limited company, as he needed to raise additional cash for expansion. This he managed to do by raising over £86,000 (£8.5 million today). In 1870 William acquired six acres of land around the Broad Oaks site, and two years later the foundry went in to full production of steam winding engines. Six years later, in 1878, the rest of the works were finally finished. The delay was put down to a river running alongside the business having to be straightened. During excavations a seam of brick-making sand was found, so the Olivers opened their own brick works. In 1878, rock boring machines, water works engine pumps, boilers, and girders were produced in many tens of thousands of tons. Edward Eastwood by 1879 had become the chairman of Oliver and Company Limited and William Oliver the managing director. One presumes that it was Edward Eastwood who provided the finances for Oliver's expansion at some point in the 1870s. It should be remembered that Edward Eastwood himself had only started his carriage and wagon works in 1863, although by this time it had been a great success and had earned him a small fortune. As we have previously learnt, he also provided the financing for his nephew Edwin Samson Moore's Midland Vinegar Company in 1874. Whatever the means of the finance, Edward Eastwood's daughter Mary Louise had married William Oliver's son John by the 1880s.

The business continued to flourish into the next few years, and by 1881 they employed over 250 staff, with wages totalling £25,000 (£2.5 million) annually. By 1885 the Olivers were listed with the Admiralty, and their business was a very large concern.

1886, however, would see a complete turn-around in the fortunes of the company. A slump in the coal and iron trades, the high overheads of the new factory and equipment, and delays in getting the factory up and running meant that on 27 March, 1886, Edward Eastwood, who was not only the chairman of Oliver's but also a main creditor and shareholder, instigated a high court petition, and the business was put into liquidation.

It may well have been the case that Edward, who by this time would have been in his sixtieth year and whose own business of wagon manufacturing relied largely upon the moving of coal and that industry, thought nothing more than to cut his losses. Perhaps not wishing to mothball the Oliver company in the hope that the industry would pick up in later years, he decided to sell, even though he would still have found himself indebted to the large overheads and monies still owed. His own business had been established twenty-three years previously, and although doing very well, he might have found old age a deterrent to making any more gambles in business. We should remember he had already invested heavily some fourteen years earlier in his nephew's Midland Vinegar Company. Although that business was doing very well and giving him a substantial return on his investment, he might have thought the time was right for consolidation of his business interests, not continued investment into a loss-making company.

The receiver put the company to auction. At that time it was said this was the largest property ever put to auction in Chesterfield. There was no offer made for the business. However, eventually in 1889 the whole works were sold to C. P. Markham. The company then became known as C. P. Markham & Co. Charles Paxton Markham then developed the company and expanded it into one of the largest manufacturers of coal and colliery equipment in the world.

One wonders whether in later years Edward Eastwood would think of this as the missed opportunity of his illustrious career. Had he only weathered the economic storm of those few years, this multi-million-pound company's success would have been his and John Oliver's, not Markham's. But alas, we will never know.

However, within the next two decades his nephew's Midland Vinegar Company would go on to purchase the rights for Frederick Gibson Garton's HP Sauce. Edward could bask in the knowledge that his name would go down in culinary history as the financial backer of what would become the doyen of British cuisine, a British institution, and a world-wide bestseller.

Here the Markhams must leave our story, their connections with the Eastwoods and Hasland un-besmirched. They are remembered by their kind donations of the fountain that now stands proud in Eastwood Park and those grand residences Ringwood and Tapton House now given over to the public and nation at large.

And what of the Eastwoods? George Albert carried on with his various business ramifications, later being joined by other cousins to help run the wagon works. His philanthropic activities continued. Thanks to him Chesterfield has hospital wards, colleges, parks, recreation grounds, and churches, which have all benefited the townsfolk of Chesterfield immeasurably.

The children of the Eastwood family, unlike some of their industrialist associates of the time, were not consumed by the riches of their parents and did not indulge themselves in drugs, sex, or general fecklessness as did some of those generations.

George Albert Eastwood died in November 1934, leaving a will of over £28 million in 2013 values. The Eastwood wagon business was left to his niece Susan Blanche Eastwood, whose father, Edward Isaac, had died aged thirty-three in 1881 in St Petersburg. He, being the eldest son, would have been the rightful heir to his father Edward Eastwood's wagon works.

The author's grandmother, Vera Eastwood, recalled family rumour that her father, Edgar Telford Eastwood, and his brother George Albert had made a verbal pact that whichever brother succeeded the other would inherit the wagon works. Whether there was any substance to this pact was to become irrelevant when George outlived his brother. Edgar Telford died in April 1934. His brother George Albert outlived him by six months, and on his death in November 1934 it was Blanche Eastwood who inherited the business.

Blanch Eastwood, assisted by her nephew Edward Hooton, continued to run the Eastwood empire until her death in 1963. When she died she was described as the richest woman in Chesterfield, and her will reveals that she left in today's money the equivalent of £14 million, a noticeable difference from when her uncle George Albert died in 1934 and her grandfather Edward Eastwood in 1910. Although the amount she left in 1963 was half as much again as her uncle did, inflation and the huge death duties introduced by the Labour government of that decade had eaten into its worth.

On Blanche's death and with the demise of wagon building and the previous nationalisation of the railways in general, the Eastwood wagon works became incorporated within her nephew's business, trading as Hooton and Green. This brought to an end over a century of the Eastwood Wagon Works.

This in-depth history of the Eastwood family provides context for the future success of Edward Eastwood's nephew Edwin Samson Moore and their Midland Vinegar Company. Our story must leave the twentieth century of the Eastwoods' demise and return back to those early days of 1874, when Edwin Samson Moore had managed to persuade his Uncle Edward to invest in his business.

FOR REPAIRS
APPLY TO
E. EASTWOOD
CHESTERFIELD
LD

EDWARD EASTWOOD
RAILWAY WAGON & WHEEL WORKS
CHESTERFIELD

MIDLAND VINEGAR COMPANY.
SEAL
TRADE MARK
BREWED from Selected MALT

(4)

The Midland Vinegar Company

With the Eastwood finance now guaranteed, early in 1874 Samson's business gathered pace. He registered his brewery as The Midland Vinegar Company, Tower Road, Aston. The original capital of the company was £1,050 (£83,000).

His first acquisition was the brewery of the Birmingham branch of the Cambrian Vinegar Company of Elland Road, Leeds, which he had originally helped to establish. This was acquired for the sum of £975 (£77,000).

In May 1874 a partnership deed was executed between Edwin Samson Moore, Alderman Edward Eastwood, J. P., of Chesterfield (his uncle), and George Humphrey Diement, with a capital of £5,200 (£411,000). This was divided into twenty-six shares of £200 (£15,750) each, Edward Eastwood taking fifteen, Edwin Samson Moore ten, and George Humphrey Diement one. This began the official trading of the Midland Vinegar Company.

Samson Moore continued his association with W. Pink & Sons Portsmouth and took up agencies from other companies for jelly crystals, custard powder, and gravy browning, all proving popular with the public.

As Samson built up his trade with various outlets throughout the area, his own brewery was being built with equal expediency. The work at his new brewery was very intense: building work was done, boilers were positioned, and steam engines and pumps were fitted.

The earliest document relating to the Midland Vinegar Company that has come to light is the following from the *London Gazette* (13 April, 1875):

Notice is hereby given that the Partnership heretofore subsisting between us the undersigned, Edward Eastwood, Edwin Samson Moore and George Humphry Dunent, carrying on business at Tower Road, Aston, Birmingham, as Brewers of and Dealers in Vinegar, under the style or firm of the Midland Vinegar Company, has been this day dissolved, so far as concerns the said George Humphry Dunent, by mutual consent. All debts due to and owing by the said firm will be received and paid by the said Edward Eastwood and Edwin Samson Moore, who will in future carry on the said business on their own account.—Dated this 7th day of April 1875. Edward Eastwood. Edwin Samson Moore. George Humphry Dunent.

A Midland Vinegar Document dated 30 September, 1924, discussing the history of the Midland Vinegar Company states that in April 1876, Mr Dunent was bought out of the company and received a bonus for his share. One presumes that a year after the *London Gazette* notice was issued was regarded as the period of time to lapse before dissolution was legally finalised. The author can find no further history of Mr Dunent, but he may have been a family solicitor who was employed to register the company and was initially acting as the company secretary.

With the Midland Vinegar Company now legally defined as under the ownership of Edward Eastwood and Edwin Samson Moore, and with the daily routine of business expansion taking up an ever-increasing portion of Samson's working day, it was time to move closer to the works. Samson decided to move his wife, Mary, and their family from Hunters Vale, Hockley Hill, to 234 Tower Road. Mary was initially displeased to find her new home right next door to the brewery, but she was won over by her husband's confidence, abundant energy, and enthusiasm, which were all now needed. The brewery building was now finished, and it was time for the process of vinegar brewing to begin.

Edwin Samson Moore's 1875 brewery as seen from Upper Thomas Street and to the left Tower Road.

Samson's brewery began production using the vinegar from Cambrian acetifiers as the necessary "starter". This was made possible by having previously bought the Birmingham branch of the Cambrian Vinegar Company. Vinegar brewing in 1875 was a long, critical process, requiring vigilant control, as Samson knew only too well. He had studied the theory, and now was the time to put that into practice.

The process involved crushed barley with a small amount of malt. This was mixed with water, and the resulting mash was heated almost to the boiling point by steam passing through copper coils. When starch of the barley had been gelatinised, the mash was cooled and the remainder of the crushed malt added.

The stirring of the mash by mechanical wooden agitators was continued until tests with iodine showed that all the starch had been converted into malt sugar and dextrin. The mash tun had a false bottom of slotted gun-metal plates, through which the liquor could be run off from the husk of the grain into a trough. It was pumped back over the grain until it ran clear and bright. The liquor, now known as wort, passed over a cooler into a fermenting vessel, where it was added to by further amounts resulting from the washing of the grains with hot water. Tests showed when the gravity of the brew was right for producing the correct strength of vinegar. After the temperature was checked, distiller's yeast was added to the wort and allowed to ferment. The wort, with its yeast in suspension, was pumped through cloth into a large vat. It remained there for several weeks to allow secondary fermentation to take place and the remaining yeast to collect at the bottom.

The yeast in the presses, which were similar to those in use in some clay industries, was scraped from the cloths with wooden scrapers and mixed with clean, cold water. It was again pumped in hessian bags for sale.

The separated wort, after the period in the large vat, was ready to be turned into vinegar using what was known as the "quick" process. For this, a starter of vinegar from a working acetifier was necessary. As discussed previously, the Cambrian Vinegar Company was the provider. This starter contained the vinegar organism which, in the presence of air, converts an alcoholic wort into vinegar. The acetifer was a round vat with a wooden staging inside about four feet from the base. Immediately below the staging, holes were drilled to allow the entrance of air. On the staging, layer after layer of birch twigs (bosoms) were laid to provide maximum surface for the mixed wort and starter to trickle over. They collected at the bottom of the vat, having been exposed during the journey to rising currents of air from the holes beneath the staging. The liquid was pumped continuously from the bottom of the vat and sprayed evenly over the birch by the rotating sparge arm.

If the temperature was right, the process would be finished in about four days. The temperature could be controlled by a tinned copper coil carrying hot or cold water. The newly made raw vinegar was then pumped to maturing vats, and about one quarter was left to act as starter for the next charge. In the maturing vats was a deep layer of beech chips, obtained from the saddlers at Walsal.

The vinegar was circulated from the bottom of the vat to the top, so that the chips of wood, acting as a filter, removed most of the cloudiness. After a final filtering, the vinegar was ready for despatch in five-gallon barrels. Stabling for up to eight horses had been built at the rear of the brewery to house the horse and drays that were used as the best form of transport until two decades later, when motorised vehicles came into production.

A typical mash tun showing the silo where ingredients were poured into the tun and also the wooden agitators used to stir the mash, which was also turned in the tun mechanically by wheel.

An early Midland Vinegar trade plate now on display at the Beamish Centre, Northumberland.

These were often to be seen in the Victorian fish and chip shops as a backdrop to the sales counter, advocating the quality of this now-readily-available condiment that was liberally splashed over the eager customers' fish and chips.

The aroma now engulfing Aston Cross was a familiar part of life for the local residents, who became immune to the vapours. Samson's brewery was not alone in the production of vinegar, as there were already several other well-established family concerns: Thompsons (Holbrook's) based in Ashted Row, Gammons of Constitution Hill, and Faradons in Glover Street.

Samson's foresight had taken into consideration the possible competition. His knowledge of the making and selling of vinegar and its inevitable potential for the future meant that his venture excelled.

The history of vinegar dates back to the ancient Egyptians. Samson had done his homework well on the subject, and he knew that the vinegar brewing techniques used today had begun as far back as the seventh century in Japan.

Vinegar is believed to have been made first by the Babylonians in 5000BC. According to Old Testament records, however, the first written account of vinegar use was in Israel as far back as 1250BC. Originally, rice vinegar was introduced from Sake. In the sixteenth century large scale production of rice vinegar began.

The name "alegar" coupled with the French for sour wine ("vin aigre") has given us the more popular name known today.

Throughout the ages vinegar had increased in popularity, and with the armed forces amongst others increasing the consumption, Samson knew that the value of this commodity could only increase. With hindsight, his theories proved right. Fishing had become a long-distance affair, with catches kept fresh by ice. The much-improved transport network meant that fresh fish, and fried fish in particular, would soon be as common as the everyday oyster stalls had been.

Served with a liberal portion of fried potatoes, another great British dish had arrived: fish and chips. It is reputed that the inventor of the recipe was a Mr Dyson from Oldham, Lancashire, around 1866. Salt had long been a condiment for spicing up a meal, and vinegar would only add to this improvement.

Samson's brewery and the other vinegar establishments were not alone in creating the aromatic vapours in Aston. Indeed, Samson's barley and malt suppliers, the Ansells of nearby Park Road, contributed to the powerful smell. Aston Cross had a close business community, and the Ansells' and Moores' association meant they and their children became firm friends.

Joseph Ansell & Sons
Brewers
Maltsters &
Hop Merchants
Aston Brewery
Maltings
Aston, Birchfields,
and
Handsworth:
Moseley Rd & Darwin St
Birmingham
Birmingham. April 1887
Head Office & Wine & Spirit Department,
PARK ROAD, ASTON.

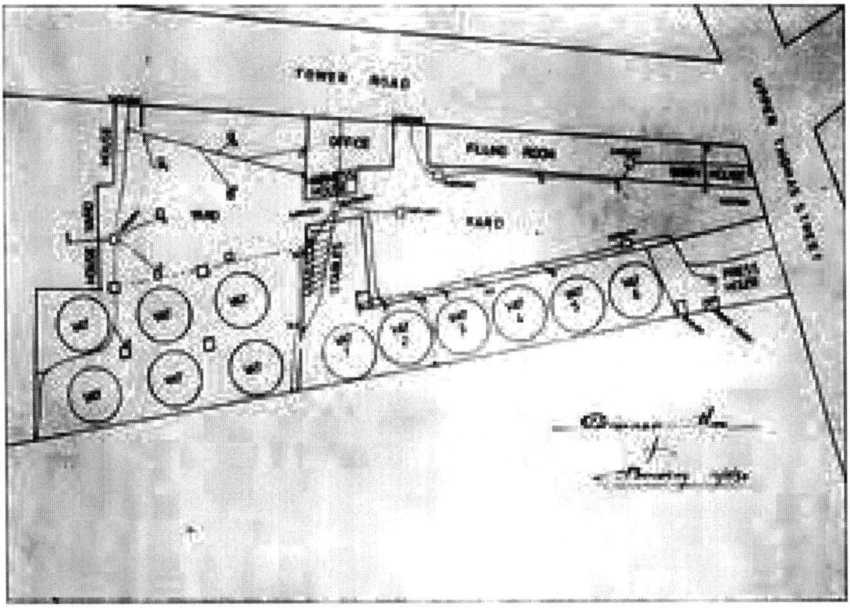
TOWER ROAD
OFFICE
YARD
YARD

Samson's business expanded rapidly, and the following plan drawn in 1890 shows the ground-floor layout of his brewery as built in 1875. Top left on the plan shows the Moores' residence. Their house at 234 Tower Road would be home to Edwin Samson and Mary Moore from 1874 to 1887. With new additions to their family and with more space needed at the brewery, the Tower Road house was demolished and replaced with new buildings for future vinegar expansion. Samson was now able to move his family to York Lodge on the Sutton Road, Erdington.

The last quarter of the nineteenth century around Aston Cross saw the arrival of many new businesses and concerns. A new school was built right next door to the brewery on Upper Thomas Street, and with more civic responsibility the whole area benefited from the clearing of slums. The night soil carts were replaced with the soon-to-be-familiar outside "lavvy" connected to the latest sewage drain systems, which meant a huge reduction in sickness and bad health related to poor hygiene.

Recreation was further advanced when the land surrounding Aston Hall was adopted as Aston's first public park. Queen Victoria opened the Hall as a museum in 1858. With the community in full employment, Aston Manor was becoming the centre of the industrious Midlands. With the surrounding enterprises booming, Samson's brewery in the heart of this new town was by now delivering tens of thousands of five-gallon barrels of vinegar to every part of the country by canal, road, and the ever-expanding railways. The company's letterheads proclaimed that the Midland Vinegar Company was the largest and most complete vinegar brewery in the world.

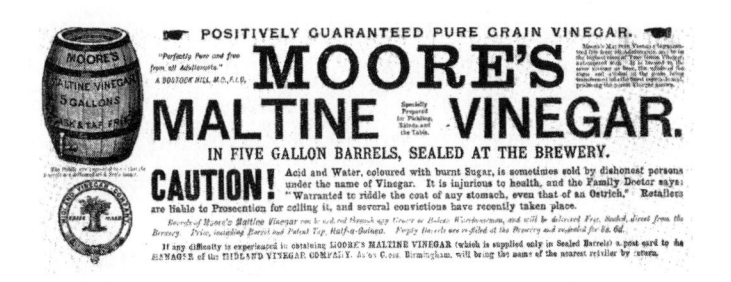

Samson Moore was a keen exponent of his products and promoted them to as wide a public as possible. Above: a newspaper advertisement from before 1890.

The Midland Vinegar Company letterhead post-1905. By this date the company proudly announced to their customers at home and around the world that they were the sole proprietors of HP Sauce, contractors to the Admirality, and the largest and most complete vinegar brewery in the world.

Samson Moore was by now bottling his own pickles. Having taken up the agencies for various products such as jelly crystals, custard powder, coffee essence, and gravy browning, his business was thriving. In 1890 his eldest son, Edwin Eastwood Moore, joined the firm. Within three years, Minnie, his eldest daughter, struck a blow for women's liberation and, despite reservation from senior family members, also joined the company doing secretarial work.

By the end of the nineteenth century, transport had expanded to reach the most important corners of the globe.

More importantly, the spice routes were accessible, thus bringing down the prices and making it more viable to use them in everyday cooking. Up to that time the traditional British meal had been wanting in added flavour; a full stomach was far more important than flavouring.

Samson, having studied the public's demand for new foods and condiments, thought the time was right for his latest venture. It was well past time to expand into sauces.

The famous cookery book of the time was by a Mrs Beeton. This inspired Samson to have various recipes developed and tested. Some looked good and smelt appetising, but the taste was not exactly what Samson was hoping for. His ambition was to bring to the masses an affordable sauce that would tempt their palate and be a complement to any meal.

With this ambition in mind, Samson Moore brought the firm's twelve sales representatives to York Lodge for a company meeting. He asked them to be aware of any new sauces on sale in shops and food outlets.

Samson was aware that it was not unusual for many homemade products to be sold in shops. Cakes and biscuits had long been handmade and helped to supplement the income of many families. Jams and pickles had also been produced in small ways or as a cottage industry, and Samson was hoping his representatives, with their vast experience, would come across a sauce that fitted his ideal as a sauce for the masses.

No doubt he offered plenty of financial incentives, and one of his twelve representatives, as we will discover, would indeed happen across a lucky find in a Nottingham grocer's store . . .

"Twelve men good and true": Edwin Samson Moore, centre front row, with his son Edwin Eastwood Moore seated to our left. This photograph was taken outside York Lodge in approximately 1894, during the company meeting at which sales representatives were alerted to be on the lookout for a new sauce.

(5)

Visitors to Aston Cross

Aston Cross was the centre of all sorts of activity during the last quarter of the nineteenth century. Not least was Aston Road, at that time the main route into Birmingham.

Four years after Edwin Samson Moore's brewery had been built, another young man, recently graduated from medical college, his career in front of him, came upon the streets of Aston in search of a rental property which his newfound status could afford. He found his house at No. 63 Aston Road, and with little more than his medical degree he soon set about the arduous task of organising the front rooms into what was to become his surgery and dispensing rooms. The soon-to-be-familiar red light was hung up in the bay window announcing to his patients that he was available for consultation. A brass plate reading "Dr A. Conan Doyle" strategically placed at eye level on the surgery wall advertised Aston's foremost medical doctor. The employees of Samson Moore's brewery soon found the surgery convenient to call upon on their way to and from work. With treatment fees costing the local inhabitants from 6d to 1/6d or, in today's money, 2p or 5p, the surgery was an added boost to this fast-developing neighbourhood. It wouldn't be until 1946 and the National Insurance Act that health care was free and doctors no longer charged.

Conan Doyle was born in Edinburgh, the third of nine children. Research shows he graduated from Edinburgh Medical School in 1875 aged twenty-six. The Birmingham civic societies have acknowledged that he lived at Aston Road from 1878 to 1881, and other research shows he practiced from this address in 1878, where he would find the local inhabitants and many of Samson Moore's employees more than eager of his services.

Conan Doyle, however, was far from content in this practice, and he applied for a post as a ship's doctor. On his acceptance, Aston was soon left without its most famous doctor and soon-to-be author. Conan Doyle would now find enough spare time to fulfil his ambition to write, and it wasn't long before his famous sleuth and other fictional characters were created.

Sherlock Holmes and the irreplaceable Doctor Watson appeared in Conan Doyle's first book, *A Study of Scarlet*, published in 1887.

The infamous Professor Moriarty, The Hounds of the Baskerville, and the many other famous characters and storylines would all arrive later to enthral the eager Victorian reader. So with his doctor's red light removed from the bay window at No. 63 and with his possessions packed away, he leaves Aston Cross and our story.

At approximately the same time as Dr Conan Doyle's first novel was published, the Aston Villa football club were celebrating their famous FA Cup victory. Like many teams of the early years of the Football League, Aston Villa was established when a group of young members of the Villa Cross Wesleyan Chapel Cricket Team were looking for possible venues to play the more popular sport of football in the autumn and spring months when the cricket season was over.

Aston Villa Football Club was established in 1874, at the same time as Samson Moore's Midland Vinegar Company brewery was being built. Two years after the football club's formation, a twenty-one-year-old George Ramsay, who had played in Scotland, was watching a Villa practice session in Aston Park. Ramsay joined in the game, and his excellent skills on the ball resulted in him being asked to join the club. It was clear that Ramsay knew more about the game than the rest of the players, and it wasn't long before he was appointed the new captain. Ramsay later commented that the team's approach to the game had been like watching eleven men dash at the opposition and have a big swipe at the ball.

This was the beginning of the famous club, and within thirteen years this fledgling team had won the FA Cup and established its name in British football.

The Aston Villa 1887 FA Cup-winning side. Back row (left to right): Frank Coulton, James Warner, Fred Dawson, Joe Simmonds, Albert Allen. Middle row: (left to right): Richmond Davis, Albert Brown, Archie Hunter, Howard Vaughton, Dennis Hodgetts. Harry Yates and John Burton are seated on the floor.

(6)

Harry Palmer's HP Sauce?

Harry Palmer was reputed to be a notorious gambler, especially at the Epsom races. It is also widely reputed that he sold the recipe for HP Sauce to Frederick Gibson Garton, a Nottingham grocer, to clear a debt he had with him. Apparently it was known as Harry Palmer's famous Epsom Sauce. But "Epsom" was widely known in its own right from the Epsom Races, so why not just call it "Epsom Sauce"? This recipe was apparently devised by Harry Palmer and thus called "HP Sauce" after his initials.

There are no documents to show the existence of a Harry Palmer having any contact with Mr Garton, nor any legal documents relating to the sale or cancelling of any debt between them. Even in the 1880s, business was not done by the word of a gentleman rather than a legal document.

If this Harry Palmer was famous, why are there no historical documents about him? Surely the racing fraternity and their magazines would have been full of the gamblers' wins and losses? More importantly, after the sale of HP Sauce in 1899, surely he would have come forward as the originator of the sauce, if for no other reason than to claim association to its eventual success.

However, in his quest to dispel myths and rumours about the origins of HP Sauce, the author has left no stone unturned in his research and has found one Harry Constable Palmer, born approximately 1860 from Chelsea/Kensington, who appears in reference to an Ellen Keeling and family from Epsom.

The Keeling's were an old, extensive family originally from the Potteries area of Staffordshire. Enoch Keeling was born 1791 in Newcastle-under-Lyme. For many years he lived in Etruria, which was the home of Josiah Wedgwood and one of his potteries. Enoch was a cashier and accountant to Wedgwood and was sometimes described as his business manager. Enoch Keeling had two sons, George Ratcliffe Keeling (born 1822) and Henry (born 1833). Both were born in the area of Etruria, Hanley, Stoke on Trent.

George and Henry came to live in Epsom, and they established a partnership called Keeling Brothers situated on Epsom High Street. The establishment was divided into a chemist shop run by Henry and a dental surgery run by George. They traded together for several years. Then their partnership was dissolved, only to see them trade separately in their respective professions. Their father, Enoch, came to live with the family in the 1870s and later died in 1880 aged eighty-nine. George Ratcliffe Keeling had a son George Radcliffe Junior, born 1853, who like his father was a dentist and practised at Ormonde House, also on Epsom High Street.

In 1888 George Ratcliffe Junior married Ellen Elizabeth Potter, born 1865. Ellen was from Epsom and the daughter of a horse racing trainer called James Potter and his wife, Elizabeth. George and Ellen's marriage was short, but they had a daughter. The marriage was an unhappy one, and Ellen took her daughter to live with her mother, Elizabeth Potter. Mrs Potter had a lodger called Harry Constable Palmer. He was apparently generally involved with the racing world as a commission agent, horse dealer, and sporting journalist.

Ellen Keeling, recently estranged from her husband, was said to prefer the company of jockeys and horse trainers. Rumours started circulating around Epsom that she and Palmer were an "item". George Keeling sent a private investigator to seek out the truth, and Ellen and Palmer were found together in a restaurant in London. One presumes the establishment had rooms. The investigator no doubt returned with the unfortunate news, and George Keeling's suspicions were confirmed.

George divorced his adulterous wife in 1894. However, Ellen and Palmer's relationship did not last, perhaps because Palmer was already married. Within a year of her divorce from Keeling, Ellen had found someone else, and that relationship resulted in marriage. Palmer disappears from our story but turns up later on the 1901 census as a boarder in Wisbech, Cambridgeshire, and again in 1911 living in Walton-on-Thames.

Harry Constable Palmer would appear in some circumstances to have the right credentials to be our HP Harry Palmer. Our research shows this man to be involved with the horse racing world. He seems a bit of a "Jack the lad" or cad, even prepared to have an affair with a married woman from an upstanding, respected Epsom family. As a journalist he was perhaps able to spin the tale, but we find no mention of him being a sauce or pickle manufacturer, although the census finds him living in lodgings in 1901 and 1911. By this time he was obviously down on his luck again, perhaps after a lifetime of living under similar circumstances of gambling, womanising, etc.

We have to consider this: would a gambler from Southern England owe a debt to a Nottingham grocer who himself owed large debts to Samson Moore's Midland Vinegar

Company and his other suppliers and as such would have no spare money to loan anyone? Would a gambler be a manufacturer of sauces and recipes? Would this so-called notorious gambler have access to and knowledge of the spices, ingredients, and techniques required for sauce brewing? Part of the legal document dated 25 May, 1899, between Frederick Gibson Garton, Edward Eastwood, and Edwin Samson Moore for the sale of HP Sauce required Mr Garton to go to the Midland Vinegar Company for one whole month after the sale and to show the Midland Vinegar employees how to mix the correct ingredients for HP Sauce as Garton himself had done, but in larger proportions.

Harry Palmer, without this knowledge of the manufacturing process of this sauce, has nothing more, if anything, than a piece of paper with ingredients. Such a document has no worth whatsoever, never mind a great enough value to be accepted as payment for an outstanding debt.

Below: a caricature of "Flash Harry" wonderfully portrayed by George Cole in the 1950s film *Girls of St. Trinian's*. This image conjures up to the author the seemingly fictitious character "Harry Palmer", reputedly the "famous Epsom Racing gambler".

(7)

HAROLD PINK'S HP SAUCE?

The Pink family now enters our story. We find Edwin Samson Moore acting as an agent and representative for them in 1871. It was previously thought that up to 1874, Edwin Samson Moore was working as a representative for an E. T. Pink pickle manufacturer of Portsmouth, which the author now believes is in fact the firm of W. Pink & Sons Portsmouth, with the following explanation about the different two companies' origins.

Thomas Pink (b. 1785) had two sons, Edward (b. 1827) and William (b. 1829). Edward lived in Bermondsley, London, where by the 1880s he had established Edward Pink & Sons, who later became known as "E. & T. Pink" when his two sons entered into partnership.

"W. Pink & Sons" was originally established by William Pink (b. 1829) during 1858 at 112 Commercial Road, Portsmouth. William was now based in Portsmouth, as was the majority of the Pink family. By 1866 the business was firmly established, so the business was incorporated into W. Pink & Sons. Later in 1887 William took his three sons into partnership with him: Ernest, Victor, and Harold.

William Pink was knighted in 1891. The partnership was changed into a limited company in 1912 with Sir Harold Pink as chairman. His son Frank served as secretary. Then, after the First World War, Frank Pink became managing director of the company and expanded it into a very prosperous concern with forty-two branches. Harold Rufus Pink was knighted by Queen Victoria in 1919.

Harold Rufus Pink with his mayoralty chain. Born in 1858, he died in 1952 aged ninety-four. His lifetime covered a century that saw empire, the industrialisation of the United Kingdom, and then the beginning of our manufacturing decline.

Was this the gentleman from whom Mr Garton bought his spices? Were his initials, HP, used by Mr Garton as an acronym for his latest sauce when keeping his shop documents separate from his sauce-making activities?

Let's presume that Mr Garton was the inventor of HP Sauce. The sauce required ingredients that would have been imported: ginger from Africa, pepper from Asia, cloves from Zanzibar, tamarind, coriander, etc. Where did Mr Garton purchase all these spices and ingredients from? His vinegar, which is the main ingredient of the sauce, came, as we know, from the Midland Vinegar Company. The rest of his ingredients would have come from a spice merchant.

By 1890, W. Pink & Sons were importers of spices and manufacturers of pickles. More importantly, Edwin Samson Moore had taken up the Birmingham agency for Pinks, so we could presume one of three options: that Mr Garton was buying all his ingredients from Samson Moore & the Midland Vinegar Company, that he was buying spices directly from W. Pink & Sons, or that he was using Edwin Samson Moore as an agent of W. Pinks, who took commission on sales he made.

By 1890, Harold Pink had become chairman of Pinks. Is it not possible, given the other options as discussed for the sauce being called HP and after considering these other similar dubious connections, that Mr Garton thought nothing more than to use the initials for his sauce from his main supplier of spices and ingredients, one Harold Pink?

Mr Garton ran his grocer's during the day. He went round the streets of Nottingham by night selling his wares for extra income and as a side line was inventing and producing sauces. To keep his sauce business separate, wouldn't it be considered good business practice to label all records, documents, costs, etc. for his sauce production under the name of the supplier, i.e., Harold Pinks Ingredients . . . HP Sauce?

Edwin Samson Moore was a representative of Pinks Pickles of Portsmouth in 1874.

(8)

HOUSES OF PARLIAMENT AND HP SAUCE?

No tome about HP Sauce could possibly be complete without a mention of the product's famous label and in particular the use of the image of the Houses of Parliament. Although the whole building itself is commonly thought of and known as the Houses of Parliament, it is in fact a part of the Palace of Westminster.

Located in the City of Westminster, the Palace of Westminster, viewed from across the River Thames. Westminster Bridge in the foreground with the Elizabeth Tower to the right housing one of five bells, the largest being "Big Ben".

The Palace of Westminster is the meeting place of the House of Commons and the House of Lords, the two houses of the Parliament of the United Kingdom. Commonly known as the Houses of Parliament after its tenants, the palace lies on the Middlesex bank of the River Thames in the City of Westminster, in Central London.

The original building, the Old Palace, was a medieval building which was destroyed by fire in 1834. A replacement building, the New Palace, stands today. For ceremonial purposes, the palace retains its original style and status as a royal residence.

On 16 October, 1834, a fire broke out in the palace. It was reputed that the fire originated in a stove which was used to burn the Exchequer's stockpile of tally sticks. The stove overheated and caught fire. It may well have been that the flue lining was also blocked with decades of soot and tar which ignited. Both Houses of Parliament were virtually burnt to the ground. Westminster Hall survived along with the Jewel Tower, the Undercroft Chapel, the Cloisters, and Chapter House of St Stephen's.

After the fire, King William IV suggested the use of Buckingham Palace as a temporary site for Parliament to meet. He had never liked the Palace and thought this a good opportunity to rid himself of the place. Parliament didn't think it was suitable and rejected his offer. Westminster had always been the chosen place for politicians to carry out their business, so it was decided to use temporary accommodation. The Painted Chamber and White Chamber were repaired immediately, and the House of Commons and Lords were able to use these buildings from as early as February, 1835.

The committee in the House of Lords announced in June 1835 that "the style of the new buildings should be either Gothic or Elizabethan". A decision was made and the foundation stone was laid in 1840. The Lords Chamber was completed in 1847 and the Commons Chamber in 1852 Although most of the work had been completed by 1860, construction was not finished until a decade afterwards.

The chosen design for the Palace of Westminster was the Perpendicular Gothic style, which was popular during the fifteenth century and returned during the Gothic revival of the nineteenth century. Westminster Hall, which was built in the eleventh century and survived the fire of 1834, was incorporated into the design.

The Palace of Westminster has three main towers. The largest and tallest is Victoria Tower, which occupies the south-western corner of the palace. Called "King's Tower" after the then-king, William IV, the Victoria Tower was completed in 1858. At the base of the tower is the Sovereign's Entrance, used by the monarch whenever entering the palace to open Parliament or for other state occasions.

The Victoria Tower houses the three million documents of the Parliamentary Archives. These include the master copies of all Acts of Parliament since 1497 and important manuscripts such as the original Bill of Rights and the death warrant of King Charles I. At the top of the cast-iron pyramidal roof is the flagstaff, from which flies the Royal Standard (the monarch's personal flag) when the sovereign is present in the palace. On the days when either House of Parliament is sitting and on designated flag days, the Union Flag flies from the mast.

The Elizabeth Tower.

The Elizabeth Tower has become synonymous with Big Ben, the heaviest of the five bells it houses. It is only slightly shorter than the Victoria Tower but much slimmer. It houses the Great Clock of Westminster, which has remained consistently reliable since it entered service in 1859.

The time is shown on four dials, which are made of milk glass and are lit from behind at night. Five bells hang in the belfry above the clock. The four quarter bells strike the Westminster Chimes every quarter hour. The largest bell strikes the hours. It is officially called "The Great Bell of Westminster" and it is generally referred to as "Big Ben", a name which is synonymous with the building itself.

A famous attempt to breach the security of the Palace of Westminster was the failed Gunpowder Plot of 1605. The plot was a conspiracy among a group of Roman Catholic gentry to re-establish Catholicism in England by assassinating the Protestant King James I and replacing him with a Catholic monarch. The conspirators placed large quantities of gunpowder beneath the House of Lords, which Guy Fawkes agreed he would detonate during the state opening of

Parliament on 5 November, 1605. If successful, the explosion would have destroyed the palace, killing the king, his family, and most of the aristocracy. However, the plot was discovered, and most of the conspirators were either arrested or killed while trying to evade capture.

The survivors were tried for high treason in Westminster Hall, convicted, and gruesomely executed by hanging, drawing, and quartering. Since then, the cellars of the palace have been searched by the Yeomen of the Guard before every state opening of Parliament, a traditional precaution against any similar attempts against the sovereign. In more recent times, 5 November has been celebrated by the building of bonfires with a homemade effigy of Guy Fawkes being perched high at the top and ceremoniously burnt. Fireworks have added to this autumnal tradition.

Another longstanding British institution using the initials HP and the logo of the Houses of Parliament is *Private Eye*. The magazine celebrated its fiftieth Anniversary in 2011. The first issue appeared on 25 October, 1961. The satirical and current affairs bimonthly magazine was conceived to expose political and celebrity indiscretions. It is a critique of both public figures and the establishment. The present editor is Ian Hislop, who has been with the magazine for over thirty years, twenty-five as editor.

The political page, HP Sauce, appeared in the magazine beginning in 1970. It was appropriately named, apparently, after the famous sauce. At that time Mary Wilson the wife of the prime minister of the day, said of her husband, "Harold will insist on covering everything with HP Sauce". He would later refute this claim, saying it was the more upmarket Lea and Perrins he preferred.

Perhaps it was thought HP "Sauce" was an appropriate name for the goings-on in the Houses of Parliament, which the *Eye* would like to expose and ridicule. Auberon Waugh, the first political correspondent of *Private Eye*, had hoped for a press gallery ticket to the Commons. When faced with opposition from the established Lobby journalists, who didn't like the idea of these new upstarts, he responded by establishing the HP Sauce column. It soon became the heart of the magazine, featuring a satirical Westminster parallel universe where fictitious characters would introduce the reader into the incompetent, murky, grubby, often self-important Westminster Village.

From September 1973 the column took a more serious course when it took the form of a more accurate, factual column where various authors were invited to contribute. Needless to say, over the years many politicians have recognised the traits of their fellow MPs, to the delight of some and disdain of others.

Humour, politics, and a favourite sauce all combined . . .

The acronym HP, we find, was therefore reputed to stand for "House of Parliament" because Mr Garton had heard that his sauce had been used by members of parliament in the restaurants of Westminster.

We ask ourselves, did the average person of the 1880s outside London know of the Houses of Parliament restaurants? Were those restaurants notorious establishments of eating, like the Savoy or other famous eateries of the capital? Would a Nottingham grocer producing as a side line a few bottles of sauce have the contacts to see his sauce sold in Parliament?

The reasoning for why the author concludes HP is not named after the Houses of Parliament is to be found in the original explanation as to why the sauce was so named. It is claimed from various sources that "Mr Garton had *heard* his sauce had been seen in the restaurants of the Houses of Parliament". So we are led to believe, then, that after that time he decided to name his sauce "HP Sauce"? So what was Garton's sauce called before it was seen in the Houses of Parliament restaurants? We are told that this unnamed sauce was seen and used in the restaurants and then named HP afterwards. How did an unnamed sauce manage to be sold to the chefs of those restaurants in the 1880s, and how? By whom? Was a chef from Nottingham, possibly a friend or neighbour of Mr Garton, working in the Houses of Parliament? Had he been into Mr Garton's shop and, having heard Mr Garton made sauces, thought no more than to offer to take some back down to London and try them out on the country's MPs? Why not, then, call it Parliament Sauce? Or Westminster Sauce? And why, we ask ourselves, did this person who apparently introduced the sauce via Mr Garton to those restaurants not come forward to claim his part?

Much speculation has been given about the name, and that has only been given more credence when Mr Garton used the Houses of Parliament as a logo for the label on his bottles. This, however, was not the case at all. Mr Garton, having contacted his bottle label supplier, discussed the label format for his HP Sauce. When the designer inquired about the name of the sauce, Garton repeated his story of how one of his sauces had been seen in a restaurant at the Houses of Parliament. Within minutes the designer suggested a picture of the Houses of Parliament as the label. Mr Garton had no need to go into the subject of his spice supplier's accounts, and on receipt of his labels and seeing them on his bottles, who was Garton to question?

HP Sauce My Ancestors' Legacy

Once HP Sauce was manufactured at the Midland Vinegar Company, the labels were unchanged except for one detail. On the bottom of the label, the name "Garton's Arkwright Street Nottingham" was removed and replaced with "The Midland Vinegar Co., Aston Cross, Garton's HP Sauce." The label still bears Mr Garton's Arkright Street, Nottingham address.

Hand-painted enamel shop sign. These early forms of advertising were supplied by the manufacturers. Erected high up on the side of the shop building, they proclaimed to the eager consumer the latest products available.

(9)

Garton's HP Sauce?

Frederick Gibson Garton was born in 1862. His father, William, was a publican, and we find the family living at the Royal Oak, Nottingham Road, New Basford, Nottingham when Frederick was working as a grocer's apprentice in 1881, aged nineteen.

The Royal Oak, Nottingham, on the corner of Sandon Street.

There is very little information about Frederick Gibson Garton's early career, but his work as a grocer's apprentice must have given him a good insight into life, for by the age of thirty he had his own shop in Arkwright Street. It was described as a small store or co-operative.

Victorian grocers bought goods in bulk and then decanted them into smaller weights. The term "grocer" originates from medieval times, when anyone who bought goods in bulk, or by the gross, was known as a grocer. The term "gross" also refers to twelve dozen (144) items.

Dried goods such as tea, coffee, rice, flour, sugar, and salt were just some of the daily products bought by the public that the grocer would buy in bulk and then separate into smaller quantities, usually weighed out in front of the customer on the shop scales. Milk delivered by the farmer in gallon urns was then sold in quarter, half, and pint measures. Sometimes the customers would bring in a jug or other container to take away their milk in. Shopping in Victorian times was a daily routine for the woman of the house. With no fridges or freezers, food was bought to be eaten and used more or less straight away.

A typical scene found in a Victorian grocer's.

Mr Garton was obviously an ambitious man, for not only was he prepared to work long, arduous hours in his shop but in the evenings he would think nothing of loading up his three-wheeled basket cart or old, rickety wooden hand cart and push them around the local back-to-back (*Coronation Street*—style) terraced houses of Nottingham to carry out his daily deliveries to the elderly and heavier orders for his regular customers.

Above: Frederick Gibson Garton in his retirement.

Below: Victorian back-to-back row of terraced houses that would form the customer base of Mr Garton's business.

Above: A typical hand cart that Mr Garton would use to deliver goods to his customers' homes. Ideal to carry heavy items such as bags of potatoes and flour.

Owning a grocer's shop in Victorian Britain was not necessarily a profitable business. The customers Mr Garton sold his goods to were the low-waged working class, whose income meant they often lived "hand to mouth" and relied upon credit, or "tick", to get themselves and their families through the working week. Terms such as "put it on the slate" were as a direct result of Victorian poverty. The term itself means literally to chalk the debtor's name and the item's cost on a board, in this case a slate.

Times were tough for the local inhabitants, and the grocer had his own bills to pay, so finding other means of an income was always on the mind of Mr Garton. In the Victorian era there were no health and safety or food standards as such. Standards for storing foods were carefree, and space being at a premium, goods came into the shop, were stored to one side, and then were sold. Cutting of meat, poultry, and fish was done at the rear of the shop on a butcher's wooden block or marble tops.

Mr Garton's shop was no different. However, he had long been interested in pickles and jams, making them as a side line and experimenting with various spices and ingredients that became available to him from travellers around the country, who would come into his store trying to introduce new products into the grocery trade. In the back of Mr Garton's shop was a "copper". These had various uses, including the boiling of clothes, meat, or hams. A traditional copper would be of brick construction with a centre where a bucket type vessel would be placed, usually made of cast iron but occasionally of copper, hence the name. These coppers were heated by a fire underneath, and a chimney took the fumes away out of the building.

Mr Garton used what little spare time he had to experiment with recipes for various sauce concoctions. In the early Victorian period, food was fairly bland. It was basic, and for most working-class families a full stomach was more important than a sprinkle of flavouring. Potato and bread-based foods were the main diet for the masses. Potato and other vegetables as a stew with bread and dripping was the norm for many, with the occasional meat dish in the week or on a Sunday.

By the final decade of the nineteenth century, wages had increased, and there were more products to choose from. Many women had found ingenious ways to make food go further. Onions were pickled, jams were made, and homemade bread, cakes, pies, and meat recipes, thanks to Mrs Beeton's ingenious cooking book, had become available for most homes' larders.

Mr Garton had a copper installed at the rear of his Arkwright shop, and for several years he made cheaply priced sauces in relatively small quantities. He pickled beetroot and onions, made jams, and sold them to subsidise his shop's income. He obviously had quite a talent for blending ingredients and came up with several recipes which were made into sauces. There was Sandon Sauce, Banquet Sauce, Nottingham Relish, Yorkshire Sauce, Worcestershire Sauce (not the original made by Lea and Perrins), Daddies Sauce, and HP Sauce.

The earliest document relating to HP Sauce that we know of is to be found when Mr Garton wrote down his secret HP Sauce recipe in his 1894 grocer's diary.

The rear of 47 & 49 Sandon Street in 2001, the site of Frederick Gibson Garton's sauce and pickle factory in the mid-1890s.

HP Sauce My Ancestors' Legacy

Below: Mr Singh with one of the very few remaining original bottles of Garton's HP Sauce. Unfortunately, he "cleared the cellar out" of all the original Garton bottles, labels, and sauce-manufacturing paraphernalia when he moved into the property at Sandon Street during 1986. Apart from the financial loss (apparently an original 1890s Garton's bottle can sell for approx. £100), the historical loss of the forensic evidence of the possible birthplace of HP Sauce is considerable.

Frederick Gibson Garton, as part of the 1899 agreement with Eastwood & Moore, transferred ownership to them of HP Sauce, Daddies Favourite, Nottingham Relish, Sandon Sauce, Worcestershire Sauce (not the original by Lea & Perrins), Banquet Sauce, and Yorkshire Sauce.

Mr Garton manufactured various sauces, all originally ideas that he thought would be acceptable to the palate of the Victorian working class. Sandon Sauce was named after the street where he lived, 47-49 Sandon Street. "Daddies Sauce", as he called it, was developed as a direct result of using ingredients that were less expensive and more easily available, especially when his "usual" suppliers were later to withhold credit. Daddies Sauce is similar to HP Sauce, but without tamarind or tomatoes and with less malt vinegar but more spirit vinegar. The name "Daddies Sauce" originated from Frederick Gibson Garton's need to distinguish between his HP and cheaper version sauce. After its conception, "Daddies sauce" was the one the Garton family experimented with on their own food. When Garton Junior asked his mother for more, he was given a quick retort, "No, leave it alone, it's Daddy's sauce." The name stuck. The Midland Vinegar Company changed the name to Daddies Favourite in 1906.

John Garton with his father's sauces: HP Sauce and Daddies Sauce (Daddies Favourite), and also a "special edition" miniature bottle to celebrate one hundred years of the Midland Vinegar Company in 1975.

The author wrote to Mr John Garton in 1987 to give him the opportunity to put his family's side to the reasons his father sold HP Sauce and the rest of his sauce business to the author's ancestors, Messrs Eastwood and Moore. His reply does not give the reader any explanation but shows that even some ninety years later, the agreement between Mr Garton and Eastwood & Moore is not quite as straightforward as we have been led to believe.

GARTON, JOHN FREDERICK.

May 1st/87.

To Mr Nigel Gregory Britton
St Erth, Hoyle, Barnwell

Dear Mr Britton,

In reply to your letter of 16 April/87, I have in my safe all the original recipes and contracts re HP Sauce, and in confirmation am sending to you a few copies. One cannot be responsible for the deeds their ancestors carried out, but as you must appreciate the Eastwoods and the Moores – did not quite "Play the Game" with my father. Nuff said –

The Nottingham Evening Post some time ago look up the story. I am enclosing a copy and you will now understand my views on the matter.

Sincerely,
John Garton.

Dear Mr Britton

In reply to your letter of 16th April 1987, I have in my safe all the original recipes and contracts re HP Sauce, and in confirmation I am sending to you a few copies.

One cannot be responsible for the deeds their ancestors carried out, but, as you must appreciate the Eastwoods and Moores, did not quite "Play the Game" with my father, enough said.

HP Sauce My Ancestors' Legacy

> *The Nottingham Evening Post, some time ago took up the story. I am enclosing a copy and you will now understand my views on the matter.*
>
> *Sincerely, John Garton.*

In his letter to the author, John Garton told of how the *Nottingham Evening Post* of Wednesday, 15 January, 1986, took up the story of the origins of HP sauce from Frederick Gibson Garton's son, John Garton. Incensed by a small coffee table book written by the actor Dinsdale Landen and his wife, Jennifer Daniel, first published in 1985 entitled *The True Story of HP Sauce*, he felt compelled to write to the authors and their publishers to put the matter right. Having had no response, he contacted the *Nottingham Evening Post*, who took up his story.

> *For years Mr John Garton has lived with the knowledge that his father never received the credit he deserved for devising the original recipes for the legendary HP and Daddies Sauces.*
>
> *Mr Garton who is 75 and lives with his wife in East Bridgford was content to let the matter fade into history—until actor Dinsdale Landen and his actress wife Jennifer Daniel decided to venture into prose to "uncover the real story".*
>
> *Their version of the events does no justice to Frederick Gibson Garton who, whatever story you wish to believe, was the undisputed brains behind the stuff we pour over our eggs and bacon each morning*
>
> *"Everybody in Nottingham knew he invented HP Sauce. But the old man wouldn't speak about it with anyone because it had gone to the Midland Vinegar Company", said Mr Garton, who was even nicknamed "HP" during his days at Nottingham High School.*

"As far as I was concerned, it was history and that was the end of it. But now I think the record should be put straight."

The *Evening Post* goes on to say that had the authors taken the trouble to consult Mr John Garton, then they might have found out. And that historic 1899 agreement shows that the Moores certainly did Mr Garton no favours. John Garton went on to explain in the newspaper item his thoughts on the subject.

"It was always a mystery to the family as to why the old man got rid of HP Sauce. The subject of HP Sauce was forbidden at home. The old man would never have a bottle in the house. But during my school days I was referred to as "HP" far more often than my own name. Almost everybody in Nottingham seemed to know about my father and HP and Daddies Favourite Sauces. But at home the subject was absolutely forbidden. Why was HP Sauce sold? I asked many times, only to incur my father's wrath. The only conclusion I finally came to was that my father must have wined too well one day and sold out. If HP Sauce was ever mentioned he seemed very upset. But we now know that Moore came along with the intention of robbing the old man of HP Sauce and did so."

The secret ingredients of the original HP Sauce were written by Mr Garton in his 1894 diary. They included garlic, shallots, ground mace, tomato puree, cayenne pepper, ground ginger, raisins, flour, and salt—as well as vinegar.

"My father was slow with his payments for the vinegar he needed to make HP Sauce and because of this he was forced to sell not only his sauces but also his name. He was a kind, proud gentleman, obviously no match for Samson Moore."

Mr Garton cites as evidence the 1899 document his father had to sign, which transferred his business and which also deprived him of any rights to carry on any trade connected with sauces and chutney.

"He was at their beck and call", said Mr Garton Junior. "He had to go over to teach them how to make it, and his expenses were limited to no more than £1 a day."

From the date of that agreement on 25 May, 1899, the HP success story gathered pace. Mr Garton concedes that the Midland Vinegar Company did a brilliant job in promoting the product. Afterwards his father initially struggled, but he eventually made a new name for himself in the provision trade, dealing chiefly in Stilton cheese, before he died aged eighty in 1942.

"My father could never have marketed HP like the Midland Vinegar Company did. They built it up to what it is today and I still eat it myself, but to insult the man who invented it . . ."

In conclusion to the newspaper article of 1986, Mr John Garton said that now, more than eighty-five years after his father had given up the secrets behind what was to become a legend, Frederick Gibson Garton's part in the events has at least been placed on record, and that is all Garton Junior wanted.

(10)

Mary Moore's HP Sauce?

There are some who have speculated even that Edwin Samson Moore's wife, Mary, was responsible for the concoction of the sauce and it was then combined with the initials "HP" and Garton's name. The author would be delighted to claim his great-great-grandmother was the "cook that spoilt Mr Garton's broth!", but alas, it's not so.

When Samson's new brewery was under construction in 1875, he moved his family from Hunters Vale, Hockley Hill, to No. 234 Tower Road, right next door to his brewery. It wasn't until 1887 that Samson bought the imposing York Lodge and Mary could be away from the smells of Aston Cross.

Home for Mary Moore was York Lodge, Erdington, from 1887 to 1930, when she died. During the early years of this period, she had another two children. York Lodge was a large, detached "mansion house" situated on the Sutton Road, Erdington. During the latter part of the nineteenth century, Erdington was a rural retreat for Birmingham's well-to-do factory and mill owners, a pleasant, tree-lined avenue of detached residence of some acclaim where the author's ancestors, the Eastwoods and the Brittons, lived alongside the Moores.

It was a delightful, tranquil place to which their families could escape from the hustle and bustle of New Aston life. Aston Cross in the last quarter of the nineteenth century was a fast-developing New Town where such establishments as Tranter's Gun Factory and Ansell's Brewery were amongst dozens of other factories and concerns that the eager workforce from the countryside had now come to work in.

York Lodge offered Mary, Samson, and their growing family the air of respectability and standing and the comfort and security that Samson's Midland Vinegar Company had provided since its formation. They were now a part of the well-established middle class of Victorian Britain.

The grand house stood alone in several acres of mature grounds. It was approached by a long gravelled carriage drive flanked by mature trees and shrubs. There were outbuildings for the carriages and stables for the horses, including Samson's favourite, Daisy. There were tennis courts and an orchard with apple and pear trees in abundance, all in a peaceful, rural idyll. The house was a sound nineteenth-century manor house of some considerable charm and size, offering spacious accommodation which included dining room, lounge, morning room, library, sitting room, billiard room, eight double bedrooms, and several single bedrooms with separate domestic quarters to accommodate the various staff of maids, cooks, boot boy, and butler. There was also Samson's man servant, Walter Russell, head gardener, Ford, under gardener, Powell and house maid Lucy Jones, all thought of as worthy, loyal members of staff, Samson would remember them in his will.

Apart from the living-in staff were those who came from the nearby Erdington village to do the day-to-day task of looking after the imposing established gardens and green houses and generally maintaining the family home.

This, then, is the lifestyle that Samson's brewery had given Mary and her family. The author finds it very unlikely that given this quality of life and surroundings, notwithstanding a still very young family to care for and with abundant servants to call upon, Mary would be found in the kitchen or scullery, sleeves rolled up around her arms, covered in spices, herbs, and vinegar, trying to concoct a special sauce for her husband's already well-established and successful business. After all, hadn't Mary just moved away from the stench of the vinegar factory and other breweries of Aston Cross after having spent over a decade amongst it all?

With Ansell's brewery directly opposite, Thompson's (Holbrooks) in Ashted Row, Fardon's in Glover Street, and Gammons in Constitution Hill, Aston Cross could never compete with the tranquillity of the Sutton Road, where the only smell and noise that would arouse the senses would be the aroma of the fields of wildflowers and the quiet interruption of birdsong.

Mary as a dutiful, typical Victorian wife and devoted mother, made sure her duties were to run a harmonious household in a manner that Samson's standing in the community now demanded, for there were guest parties and business associates to entertain. These were more than enough for Mary to occupy herself with.

Above: a typical Victorian kitchen similar to what could have been expected at York Lodge.

(11)

"Saucy Business"

With the letters of Mr John Garton and from the research carried out over the years, the author gives to the reader a version of events that would seem probable, given the circumstances and evidence known.

It was in the spring of 1899 when Frederick Gibson Garton, the Nottingham grocer, pickle and sauce manufacturer, found himself in difficult financial circumstances owing to his failure to balance his books and pay his many creditors on time.

Struggling to run his shop at Arkwright Street Nottingham during the daytime and establish his sauce and pickle manufacturing business from the rear of his home in the evenings, Mr Garton had continued to purchase stock and ingredients for both businesses, which got him further into debt.

His main creditor was Pinks of Portsmouth, who had supplied him with all his ingredients and spices for his sauce business. He had also built up a considerable debt with the Midland Vinegar Company of Birmingham, who had supplied him with their finest-quality malt vinegar for his pickles and various sauces.

Harold Pink, the managing director of Pinks, had become concerned with Mr Garton's debt. Mr Garton had been contacted many times and told this situation could not continue. His credit had already been reduced, and it was now time to clear this considerable debt before any more credit could be discussed. In his last act before taking legal action, Mr Pink contacted his old friend Edwin Samson Moore at the Midland Vinegar Company.

Samson Moore had been the Pinks Birmingham representative in 1871 some twenty-eight years earlier. He had sold spices and other ingredients of theirs and also for several other similar concerns, for in those early days in and around the Midlands Samson Moore had been making his living as a commission agent, so would he be able to exert some pressure on Mr Garton. Pinks knew the man was also heavily in debt to Samson Moore's vinegar company.

Mr Garton had already gone into production of his Daddies Sauce, a cheaper version of HP Sauce, possibly as a fall-back against what might follow if his main spice supplier were to stop his credit, for this sauce used less expensive spices and spirit vinegar, unlike the more expensive malt vinegar which was used for the HP Sauce. Samson Moore had already sent his accounts manager to Mr Garton's shop on Arkwright Street to remind him about prompt payment.

The Moores by this time had made it their business to thoroughly investigate Frederick Gibson Garton and his sauce and pickle manufacturing business. This was made possible due to Moore's representative, who served the grocers' trade and shops in and around the Nottingham area and who had passed on a dossier of information about Mr Garton's business. The Moores were now fully aware that Mr Garton was selling in relatively small quantities his various sauces to the residents of the back-to-back streets of Nottingham.

The Moores, having received this information, may have felt him a threat, for they themselves would be fully aware about the adage "from little acorns grow—". Mr Garton's fledgling sauce business was by now having quite a local success.

Ever since the conception of the Midland Vinegar Company, Samson Moore had always been on the look-out for a cheap sauce for the masses. His vinegar business was by the late 1890s of considerable size and success. His uncle, Edward Eastwood, had found his initial investment more than rewarded by the success of Samson's vinegar business. Was Mr Garton's debt with the Midland Vinegar Company overlooked? Perhaps it should be extended. Why shouldn't Mr Garton be a success? The more he produced and sold his sauces and pickles, the more demand for vinegar from the Moores would be required. At least, that's what Mr Garton may have been led to believe.

Perhaps a careful eye should be kept on Mr Garton and his sauce business while Samson Moore found time to understand exactly what had made the local inhabitants of Nottingham buy these sauces and what foods they were covering his sauce products with. This was to be an early-day feasibility study, for Samson Moore needed as much information as he could find before he made his next step.

The information Samson Moore's Nottingham salesman would reveal to him would be a true revelation. Samson had thought he had seen and heard all there was to know about sauces. It seemed that Mr Garton's sauces were a success mainly because of their price to the consumers, who had little disposable income left after settling their day-to-day bills. Mr Garton's sauces became a bit of a treat to liven up the palate of those hard-working Victorian residents. The rich, thick brown sauces gave a sharp tang to their customarily bland, basic dishes.

So it was on that fine April morning of 1899 that Samson Moore's Midlands salesman had entered Mr Garton's store on Arkwright Street to do his regular Nottingham rounds. He introduced himself as usual, enquiring of the whereabouts of the shop owner.

"Mr Garton is out delivering," said his wife. "He won't be back till later this evening. Now can I help you with anything?"

"Well, I was hoping to discuss Mr Garton's account and to see if any new orders were required."

"You will have to come back to the store and ask him later," she said. With the conversation seemingly at an end, the salesman happened to glance at the shelf directly behind Mrs Garton, on which a group of bottles was neatly assembled. His eye was immediately attracted to the ones marked "HP Sauce." With Samson Moore's earlier request to all salesmen to be mindful of any sauce on sale in shops that appeared to be new or seemed unusual still lingering in his conscience, the salesman requested to purchase a couple of these bottles of sauce and then said to Mrs Garton, "What's the HP about, then?"

"Oh, that sauce is made from one of our suppliers, Harold Pink's, ingredients, but none of the locals knows who he is. Everyone was guessing what the HP stood for, and then someone said, 'You could say it's Houses of Parliament sauce. Everyone knows that place.' And the name stuck, so we left it at that."

The salesman left the store with his new acquisition all wrapped up in brown paper and promptly made his way back to Aston Cross, full in the knowledge that a reward might be coming his way—if nothing else, surely a promotion, perhaps area sales manager. With his many years in the grocery trade, he had been instinctively alerted to the potential that this may indeed be the type of sauce Samson Moore had asked his sales team to be on the lookout for.

When he got back it was late, so he went straight to the Moores' residence at York Lodge, Erdington. He had been there only recently when Samson Moore had decided on a promotional photograph of himself, his son Edwin, and all the sales staff.

He handed the bottles of sauce to a more-than-inquisitive Samson Moore.

"Garton's HP Sauce. What's the HP stand for, then?" Moore asked.

The salesman retold Mrs Garton's explanation. In that one moment, Samson Moore tied all the information together. It all made sense. Here was his sauce, here was a supplier indebted to him, and an old friend was calling in a favour.

In April 1899, and Samson Moore, armed with the information he required about Mr Garton's sauces, decided to put his *coup de grace* into place. Pinks were contacted, and the Moores agreed to settle Mr Garton's debt on his behalf. As unusual as their request was, Pinks were not to question the whys and wherefores. Indeed, they were just satisfied to have been paid in full for this outstanding debt. No doubt Samson Moore had even managed to make some commission on the deal. With Pinks now settled, the Moores could make their next move.

The distance between the Moore's Aston Cross Midland Vinegar Company and Mr Garton's store in Arkwright Street, Nottingham, was approximately forty-five miles. In Victorian

England the road network was still sparse and in its infancy. Travelling long distance by horse and carriage was now becoming a thing of the distant past. Samson Moore and his son Eddie were to take the train from the newly built Aston Station to Nottingham and the final couple of miles by horse and carriage to Mr Garton's shop.

On arrival at Nottingham Station, they called for a carriage and soon found themselves along the back-to-back cobbled streets of Nottingham, where the womenfolk could be found cleaning windows, blacking steps, and doing the weekly wash. Sheets and clothes fluttered away, encouraged by the industrial breeze that was carried along the back yards of these typical Midland working-class homes. It was all a far cry from the rural retreat of York Lodge and the middle-class suburbia of Sutton Road.

As they approached the store on Arkwright Street, the horse and carriage made quite a spectacle. Bare-footed children with torn trousers and ripped shirts ran alongside the carriage, their faces smeared with a mixture of soot and grime. Poverty in the 1890s wasn't just found in London's Dickensian streets. Cries of "Gives us a penny, mister," were ignored, and the carriage soon came to a halt outside Mr Garton's store. Who were these visitors? Royalty? Local dignitaries? The mayor? Completely unannounced, the Moores entered the store.

This little store was to the Moores no more than just another, typical grocer's, which could be found on any back street. Here was a jumble of goods and wares and an assortment of produce. One side of the store was given over for the daily-consumed foodstuffs, and on the other side were household items such as buckets, brooms, and mops. As pleasant introductions were made to a rather shamefaced and embarrassed Mr Garton, the atmosphere soon became tense. For what had the Moores come in person to his store for, thought Mr Garton, if it wasn't to call time on his enterprise and the foreboding of the bailiffs?

Mr Garton had become the schoolboy about to meet the wrath of the headmaster. He began to think how had it all come to this, how and why he had let things slide. Was he wrong to pursue his sauce and vinegar business at the expense of delaying payment of his more important bills?

Mrs Garton must be removed from the scene of reckoning, he thought. She was asked to watch the shop while the Moores were ushered swiftly into the rear of the building.

Mrs Garton was strong and forthright. She was not short when making her feelings known to her husband, especially about her beloved shop, but like a dutiful Victorian wife she knew when to keep away from "men's business". Reluctantly, she minded the store while her husband took the Moores through the Gartons' emporium, far away from listening ears. Mr Garton offered the Moores tea and biscuits. They declined. This was not a social visit; it was a day of reckoning, a time to stand up and be counted.

"Tea? We have no time for tea, Mr Garton. There is business to hand, and I think you know why we are here, don't you? It's your account. It's long overdue, and you have debts to others, including unpaid bills to some of my business associates, which a Mr Harold Pink from

Portsmouth has personally asked me to resolve on his behalf."

Mr Garton tried to reassure the Moores that he had himself unpaid invoices from customers and that by the end of the month he expected all outstanding debts to be paid.

"Come, come, Mr Garton," said Samson Moore. "This situation has gone on far too long, and my patience is now exhausted. You have been given long enough to sort out your finances. You have taken no notice or even acknowledged Mr Pink's request for his bills to be paid. Now I find myself in this awkward position of having to make clear to you that this urgent matter must be in hand by the end of today. Now what about payment? Well!" . . .

Mr Garton sank to his knees, ashen-faced, head clasped in his hands. He was by now beginning to feel like a broken man.

"If only I was given more time—" he explained.

"More time?" said Samson Moore. "More time! Time has finally run out for you, Mr Garton. I want this situation resolved today, so what do you propose to pay me with?"

"Take what you wish from my store to the value of what is owed," said Mr Garton.

"Take what I want? And just what do you presume I will be doing with your shop stock? I am the largest vinegar producer in the world. I'm not in the business of running a costermonger's yard," said a red-faced Samson Moore.

"No, this just won't do. And anyway, your stock is unpaid. Therefore it still belongs to your suppliers. It's not yours to sell without paying the suppliers with the proceeds, now is it?

Samson, having played the bad cop, decided it was time to play the "good cop" card, so he approached the subject of the aroma coming from the rear outhouse.

"Now then, Mr Garton, what's all this brewing away in the copper?"

"That's my sauce. It's nearly ready to bottle up. I can give you as many bottles as you want once its ready," said Garton.

"As many as I want? Well, that will mean hundreds—no, thousands—to clear up your debt to me, Mr Garton, now won't it?"

Garton shrugged his shoulders in defeat and acknowledge Samson Moore's reasoning. It looked like he could never clear his debts with what he had in his store, never mind his copper.

Samson looked into the yard and, on seeing the basket cart with the poorly hand-painted sign reading "Garton's HP Sauce", enquired, "Your basket cart, Mr Garton—I take it you use it for delivering goods? And what's that sign all about, then?"

"That's the name of the brown sauce brewing in the copper," enthused Mr Garton.

"HP? Tell me, Mr Garton, why not just call it Garton's Sauce? What's the 'HP' stand for?" enquired a more-than-interested Samson Moore.

Mr Garton told Samson Moore the story of how his brown sauce had been seen in one of the restaurants of the Houses of Parliament and it followed that HP would be used.

"A likely story," said Samson Moore. "Nothing to do with my business associate's outstanding account, one Mr Henry Pink, then?"

Mr Garton stooped his head, shamefaced. He didn't respond.

"Well, whatever the name, I admire your ambitions. Back to the day's business, Mr Garton. Looks to me that you're in a pretty fine mess. The store will have to go. Your local standing as a respected shop owner is finished, and I presume your wife is not going to be too pleased about what's been going on—unless she is also implicated in these bad debts. Now, is she involved as well, Mr Garton?"

"My wife has nothing to do with the running of my sauce business. She runs the shop and deals with customers, and I am solely to blame for the debts incurred. The less my wife hears about these goings-on, the better. My marriage, family—it's going to be all over," said Mr Garton.

"It needn't get to that, Mr Garton," said Samson Moore.

For he now had Garton in the palm of his hand. Here was Garton on the verge of bankruptcy, disgrace in the local community, and shame before his wife and family—but perhaps Samson Moore could offer him a lifeline.

"I tell you what, Mr Garton. Let's see if we can rescue something from this mess. I'm a man who respects hard work and family values, but it's hard to see where I can help you without being at a loss myself. This sauce, you think it could sell on a regular basis?"

"It's been very popular with my customers around Arkwright Street and the surrounding neighbourhood, so I see no reason others wouldn't like it as well. I only use your best malt vinegar, and all the spices and ingredients are of the best quality," Mr Garton proudly announced to a more passive and interested Samson Moore.

"I can see that," said Samson Moore. "We might have some possibilities with this sauce. What other sauces and products do you make?"

Mr Garton began to perk up and talk of his Daddies Sauce, his Sandon Sauce, and his pickles, relishes, and chutneys. He went on to divulge his whole business to Samson Moore, perhaps as the last act of someone desperate to please and to salvage something from this dire situation.

Samson Moore knew what he wanted, had come for what he wanted, and was now able to put to Mr Garton his demands. "The best I can do for you, Mr Garton, is an agreement whereby I take in lieu of your debts the legal assignment of HP Sauce, all your other established sauces, pickles, and chutneys, and the trade name F. G. Garton & Co. To give your store debts a bit of assistance, I will pay you in cash £150. In return you will have cleared your debts as far as your sauce manufacturing business is concerned, you will have saved your dignity and standing in the community, and your store here in Arkwright Street will be able to continue to trade as before."

This was a sweeping proposal made before Mr Garton. It was hardly thought up on the spur of the moment, and Mr Garton probably realised this, but he was in no position to negotiate anything less. Realistically it was a better deal than he could have possibly have expected earlier that morning when the Moores entered his shop. He had now kept his store, his wife had been kept in the dark, and his sauces would still be a success, although without him attaining the kudos he thought he deserved.

Samson said, "Enough of this talk of business. Let's shake hands on the deal, and how about I take you into

Nottingham City Centre to a fine restaurant I know and let the legal people take care of the details?"

With Samson Moore's horse and carriage waiting outside the store, Mr Garton showed the Moores through the shop. With a courteous good-bye to Mrs Garton, they left for Nottingham.

Whether Mr Garton dined out too well, consumed too much fine wine, simply acted out of a great sense of relief we can only speculate, but the historic agreement of 25 May, 1899, leaves the reader in no doubt of what the Moores came for, planned, and executed.

Below page: a copy of the hand-written agreement of 25 May, 1899.

Dated the 25th of May 1899
Mr F. G. Garton to Messrs Eastwood & Moore
Assignment of Goodwill of business of Sauce & Chutney Manufacturer including 2 trade marks.

This Indenture made the twenty fifth day of May, One thousand eight hundred & ninety nine between Fred Gibson Garton, of number 47 Sandon Street New Basford & 236 & 238 Arkwright St both in Nottingham in the county of Nottingham trading under the style or firm of "F G. Garton & Co sauce manufacturer of the one part & Edward Eastwood & Edwin Samson Moore both of Tower Rd. Aston Juxta Birmingham in the County of Warwick trading under the style or firm of "the Midland Vinegar Co" Vinegar Brewers of the other part whereas the said, Fred Gibson Garton has for some years past carried on (inter alia) the trade or business of a sauce & chutney manufacturer at Nottingham aforesaid under the style or firm of "F. G. Garton & Co" & he is the registered proprietor in connection with the said business of two Trade Marks numbered respectively 99739 & 195162 in the register of Trade Marks for goods in Class 42 of the third *schedule to the Trade Marks Rules 1890. And whereas various brands of the sauce manufactured by the said Fred Gibson Garton are known by distinguishing names as follows namely "Gartons HP Sauce" "Worcestershire Sauce" "Yorkshire Sauce" "Garton & Co" "Indian Chutney" & "Daddies Favourite" And whereas the said Fred Gibson Garton has agreed to sell to the said Edward Eastwood & Edwin Samson Moore* Manufacturers together with the said Trade Marks intended to be herby assigned & together with the exclusive right to the use of the trade names of "F. G. Garton & Co" in connection with the manufacturer & sale of Sauce, Chutney & Pickles & of the names "Banquet" & "Gartons" & the Initial letters "HP" respectively forming portions of the said trade marks & also together with the several recipes or formulas for the manufacturer of the sauces & chutneys now manufactured & dealt in by the said Fred Gibson Garton & also together with all the bottle moulds now used by him in the said business but not including the book & other debts of the said business, at the price of One hundred & fifty pounds & upon pursuance of the said agreement for sale the said Fred Gibson Garton has delivered to the said Edward Eastwood & Edwin Samson Moore the said several recipes or formulas for the manufacturer of the said Sauces & Chutneys & a list of the customers with whom he has had dealings in connection with the said business And whereas it was part of the said agreement for sale that the said Edward Eastwood & Edwin Samson Moore should take from the said Fred Gibson Garton all invoice prices his stock of stationery, sauce bottle labels & other printed matter in good condition & also his stock of bottles sauce boxes & ingredients in the manufacturer of sauce as used by him in connection with the said business and also at * Gibson Garton has delivered to the said Edward Eastwood & Edwin Samson Moore the said stock of stationery bottle labels & other printed matter & also the said stock of bottles & bottle moulds in accordance with the said agreement Now this Indenture Witnesseth that in consideration of the sum of One hundred & fifty pounds to the said Fred Gibson Garton now paid by the said Edward Eastwood & Edwin Samson Moore (*

the receipt whereby the said Fred Gibson Garton as beneficial owner herby assigns unto the said Edward Eastwood & Edwin Samson Moore as part of their partnership property all the interest & goodwill of the said Fred Gibson Garton in the said trade or business of a sauce & chutney manufacturer And also the said two several trade marks and all privileges incidental thereto together with the exclusive right of the said Edward Eastwood & Edwin Samson Moore to the use of the trade names of "F. G. Garton & Co" in connection with the manufacture & sale of sauce, chutney & pickles & also of the names "Garton" & "Banquet" the initial letters "HP" forming portions of the said Trade Marks, as aforesaid respectively And Also the said several recipes or formulas for the manufacturer of said Sauces & Chutneys To hold unto the said Edward Eastwood & Edwin Samson Moore absolutely as part of their partnership property and the said Fred Gibson Garton herby covenants with the said Edward Eastwood & Edwin Samson Moore that the said Fred Gibson Garton will at the request & cost (but not * from time to time for a period of One calendar month from the date hereof attend at the place of business of the said Edward Eastwood & Edward Samson Moore at Birmingham aforesaid for the purpose of showing them & instructing their workmen or such other person or persons authorised by them for that purpose in the proper & correct process of the best & most advantageous means of manufacturing the said Sauces & Chutneys in accordance with the said several recipes or formulas And Also that the said Fred Gibson Garton his heirs executors or administrators will not at any time during a term of five years completed from the date hence either alone or jointly or in partnership with or as agent for any other person or persons & either directly or indirectly carry on or be concerned or interested in or assist any other person or persons to carry on or be concerned or obtain any interest in the trade or business of a Sauce or Chutney Manufacturer within the United Kingdom of Great Britain & Ireland And also that the said Fred Gibson Garton his heirs either alone or jointly or in partnership with or as agent for any other person or persons

& either use or indirectly use or to be party or party to the use of the said trade name of "F. G. Garton & Co" or the said names "Banquet" "Gartons" or the said initial letters "HP" respectively portions of the said trade marks respectively or the surname "Garton" either or in conjunction with other name or names herein-contained shall be deemed to exclude the right of the said Fred Gibson Garton to use the said trade names of "F G Garton & Co" or the surname "Garton" in connection with any business other than the manufacturer of Sauce, Chutneys or Pickles which he is now or may hereafter be carrying on or to be engaged or concerned in or to prevent him from carrying on or being engaged or concerned in the carrying on of the business of a Pickle Manufacturer under any other names than that of "Garton" And Also that the said Fred Gibson Garton will not at any time hereafter publish disclose discover or otherwise make known to any other person or persons the said several recipes or formulas or any of them or the nature or relative quantities of the ingredients contained or set forth therein respectively but will at all times keep the same & every portion thereof secret & undisclosed And Also that the said Fred Gibson Garton will not do or cause or suffer to be done either directly or indirectly any other act matter or thing whatever whereby the said Edward Eastwood & Edwin Samson Moore might be prevented or hindered from taking & enjoying the full benefit & advantages of the said business & the future profits & involvements arising there from this as full ample & beneficial a making as the said Fred Gibson Garton now holds & owns And the said Edward Eastwood & Edwin Samson Moore hereby covenant with the said *

Time to time & at times hereafter keep indemnified the said Fred Gibson Garton & his estate & effects from and against all liability in connection with or arising from the use by them of the said trade names In witness whereof the said parties to these presents have here unto set their hands and seals this day & year first before written.

*Signed sealed & delivered by the Fred Gibson Garton O
before named Fred Gibson Garton Edward Eastwood O
in the presence of Edwin Samson Moore O*

*Stanley Seward Bewtrudge
122 Noel St Nottingham
Commercial Traveller*

*Signed Sealed & delivered by the
Before named Edward Eastwood
In the presence of*

*James Webster Clerk
26 Tapton Terrace
Chesterfield*

*Signed sealed & delivered by the
before named Edwin Samson Moore
in the presence of*

*Minnie Moor
York Lodge
Erdington*

*Part of paragraph missing or ineligible.

To give the reader some idea of the value of £150 in 1899 we have included some of the following examples.

£150 in 1899 was equal approximately to £16,000 in 2013. The following trades and occupations show the annual wage in 1901 earned.

Teacher's annual salary: £147=50

Skilled in engineering: £116=50

Skilled in the printing trade: £92=66

Government low-wage earner: £72=20

Agricultural labourer: £41=94.

One should remember that in 1901 the 37-hour week was not around nor the minimum wage. Agricultural workers in 1901 could be expected to work an 80-hour week.

The historical agreement of 1899 clearly states that the payment of £150 from Messrs Eastwood and Moore was "Not including the book or other debts of the said business".

It should also be noted that Mr Garton didn't give up all his stock and machinery, as the legal document of 1899 demanded, for we find in 1986 a Mr Singh who purchased the old home of Mr Garton in Nottingham claiming that when he was emptying out the cellar he came across a mass of materials, bottles, and manufacturing equipment, which he disposed of in a very large skip.

Perhaps Mr Garton was hoping to continue his sauce manufacturing at a later date, or perhaps he just didn't bother to tell the Moores, as they had no knowledge of him having a factory at his home address as well as his shop.

Part of the historic agreement of May 1899 meant that Mr Garton would have to come to the Midland Vinegar Company for one whole month to show the workforce how to establish the correct methods of manufacturing the sauce and also the exact quantities of ingredients used. He was given a £1 a day for expenses or £110 in today's values, perhaps giving him slightly more than he could have expected to earn in his store, on a daily basis, in Victorian England. Over the month, this was an additional £20 [£2,200] giving Frederick Garton a total of £170 or approximately £18,000 in today's values for that 1899 agreement.

One wonders, having studied and fully understood the contract he signed, whether Mr Garton reluctantly agreed to the demands made on him by the Moores in the knowledge that all the bottles of sauce would continue to carry the name of Garton's HP Sauce. In the event, one thing was quite sure. As his son John Garton told the author in 1987, his father from that day onwards never had "the stuff in the house" and refused to talk about his reasons for selling to the Moores until much later in life.

(12)

SAMSON MOORE'S HP SAUCE

With the Moore's legal team sorting out all the final paperwork, Samson eagerly awaited the arrival of his latest acquisition to his expanding empire. The Nottingham-to-Birmingham railway had been extended to the recently built Aston Station. On that spring morning of May 1899, arriving on the 9:15 a.m. from Nottingham, stored safely in the goods carriage, was the final piece of the jigsaw to complete Samson Moore's ambition to bring a sauce worthy of the palate and at an affordable price for the masses.

Arriving at Platform Two from Nottingham, the train pulled into Aston Station. The guard opened the goods carriage and examined the contents, looking for goods, parcels, and packages for businesses and residents of Aston. He soon came across the three-wheeled basket cart with its contents carefully held together with parcel string. Bold labels attached to the cargo announced the recipient's address: *"Moore, Aston, Birmingham"*.

The guard carefully unloaded the precious merchandise. The consignment was signed for by the Midland Vinegar works manager and wheeled the quarter of a mile along the cobbled streets of Aston back to its new home at the brewery.

Once it arrived, the basket cart was ceremoniously carried up to the management offices, where it was examined by a jubilant Samson Moore and his son Eddie. This basket cart, the contents held together with flimsy parcel string, contained the makings of a sauce that Samson knew would soon satisfy even the most discontented of palates.

Although it was a small basket cart, it couldn't hide the Moores' huge ambitions. For their soon-to-be famous condiment to succeed, they knew the first thing they had to do was to source all the ingredients and spices required to manufacturer large quantities of the rich brown sauce. Unlike Mr Garton, who kept a relatively small stock of the matured sauce for his local customers from the back-to-back streets of Nottingham in his Arkwright store, the Moores intended to supply every greengrocer and food outlet in the country.

World sauce domination was a dream they could only hope to achieve in later years. Little did they know of how successful their sauce would be. Within a decade, their dream would indeed be fulfilled. For now, however, accounts were set up with suppliers. It soon came apparent that the existing brewery, as vast as it had been when built a quarter of a century before, was not going to be big enough for the additional bottling, labelling, storage, and despatch facilities that would be required.

In 1886 a close neighbour in the beer brewing industry, Alfred Homer, who had previously been in business in a small way around the corner on Park Road, had built the Vulcan brewery on the south side of Tower Road. Mr Homer was eager to expand to compete with the other similar establishments, but with competition between himself and the larger Ansells Brewery, he had found himself in financial trouble, Samson had heard from a business acquaintance that Homer might sell if things didn't improve. The brewery would be ideal as bottling plant, but for now Samson thought it best policy just to wait and see how things developed. He decided to start production of his HP Sauce on his own premises. By reorganising plant and machinery with a squeeze, they could just make do.

With Edwin Eastwood Moore now secure at his father's side running the business, Samson's eldest daughter, Minnie, who had insisted she could work as efficiently as any man, had asked her parents to allow her to follow in her brother's footsteps. Another Moore would be an added attraction to the family business, Samson thought, but in the late 1890s women's liberation in the workplace was still frowned upon. Her mother, Mary, was not so agreeable, but Samson was a proud, hard-working Victorian and saw in his daughter his own values and qualities. Despite Mary's reservations, Minnie joined the family firm.

Samson Moore, although eager to launch his HP Sauce, didn't neglect his existing vinegar business. The public would have to wait a few more years before they could have the opportunity to taste the new condiment. There were plenty of preparations to make. Apart from securing all the large stocks of ingredients, once made the sauce would have to be kept in large vats to mature before it was ready for bottling. The need for more space had become paramount, so after much thought Samson once again turned to the brewery across the road belonging to Alfred Homer. A price was agreed, and Samson now had his bottling and labelling plant. The premises were ideal not only to help with the much-needed space for bottling but for any future expansion. Once the sauce was launched, the extra space would be essential. A pipeline was laid under Tower Road connecting the Midland Vinegar brewery with the Vulcan brewery. The sauce would be pumped over to the new bottling and labelling facilities and made ready for despatch.

In 1901 Samson registered F. G. Garton Sauce Manufactory at Tower Road. The Sauce would remain known as "Garton's HP Sauce" for many years to follow, although at a later date the name "Garton's" would be dropped and the more familiar name of "HP Sauce" adopted. The soon-to-be-familiar picture of the Houses of Parliament was also registered. Samson had also taken every care to make sure that before the launch of his new sauce, not only the taste but also the bottle shape, labelling, and marketing of the product would be acceptable to the public.

The new century was dawning. The last quarter of the nineteenth century had seen the arrival of many soon-to-be familiar and commonplace inventions. The telephone and electric light bulb had made Bell and Edison household names. The motor car was in production, and the latest newspaper, the *Daily Mail*, had come into circulation at a price of 1/2d. It was to be the first of many affordable newspapers for the mass of the population. In the political field, the Labour Party was in its infancy. As dusk set on this industrious century, Samson's new sauce was waiting for the right moment for its historic launch.

Samson knew that if his sauce was to be acceptable, the public must be made aware of the quality of the sauce they were being asked to purchase from their hard-earned wages. In the last half of the nineteenth century, the general public's suspicions about the contents of foods were confirmed when public analyses were set up to test the contents and quality of manufactured foods, which they suspected of being adulterated. The Act of 1875 made it an offence to sell any food or drug which was not of the nature, of the substance, or of the quality demanded. These new standards helped to distinguish mediocre products from those produced to give the public confidence in their quality.

Birmingham's first medical officer was a Dr Alfred Hill. Samson Moore could think of no one better qualified to test the quality of his vinegar and sauces. Samson proudly proclaimed on his new labels of HP Sauce the following verdict from the doctor:

> Dear Sirs: I beg to report that I have analysed the sample of Garton's HP Sauce received from you on the 18th inst., and find it to be made from the best materials.
>
> The well known Midland Vinegar Companys vinegar, than which, in my opinion, there is no better in the market, is used in its preparation, while it is quite free from Boric or Salicylic Acids, or other preservatives. It is of pleasant and piquant flavour, and is in every respect a thoroughly Good Sauce.
>
> Yours faithfully, A Bostock Hill County Analyst.

The statement would only add to the already professional packaging of the sauce. Dr Hill's comments were fair, as the man himself was in his work. From these beginnings it can be no surprise that with his experience Dr Hill later founded his own establishment in Birmingham testing and commenting on foods and allied products. Dr Hill's firm, Messrs Bostock, Hill, and Rigby, can claim that they tested the products from Tower Road for well over a hundred years, up until 2006.

With his sauce manufacturing plant in full production, mature stocks of sauce stored in the large vats, and the bottling plants working overtime, HP Sauce was finally launched in 1903. Distributed around the country into greengrocers, fruit and vegetable shops, and all food outlets, the sauce was an instant success. Samson's meticulous planning over the previous three years of securing ingredients and producing large stocks of matured sauce was rewarded. Re-orders came in by the tens of thousands, and he was able to keep up with the demand.

The Midland Vinegar Company established in 1875 was now intensely productive, manufacturing not only HP Sauce but also all the previously established pickles and vinegars, which were still in huge demand. The products taken up from agencies in the early 1880s were now renamed and labelled using the Garton's name. So now the company was producing vinegar, HP Sauce, pickles, baking powder, table jellies, cream custard, and blancmange. The brewery was bursting at the seams. More land was purchased to build stables, blacksmith forges, carpentry shops, and buildings to store the thousands of casks of maturing vinegar.

Part of the 1899 historic agreement between Edward Eastwood, Edwin Samson Moore, and Frederick Gibson Garton for the purchase of HP Sauce also included Mr Garton's other products, all now manufactured at Aston Cross but still using the name of "Garton's" as the trade name. This made it virtually impossible for Frederick Gibson Garton to set up against the Moores by selling similar products using his own name in the future.

Samson Moore was not a man to rest on his laurels. With the immediate success of his HP Sauce, he knew that to secure his product as a universal staple ingredient in the nation's shopping basket, he had to follow up the sauce's initial success with continued marketing.

When one looks back at the history of the Midland Vinegar Company and in particular HP Sauce, one has to concede that Samson Moore was a man well before his time. For those of us today involved in marketing, the name of Satchi & Satchi is synonymous with the promotion of the world's largest organisations. In the 1980s they successfully oversaw the election campaign of Margaret Thatcher and her subsequent premiership.

Samson Moore a century earlier could of been described in the same way, for his marketing strategies were well advanced for the time. It would be no surprise when, in the pursuit of a memorable promotional tour of the country to keep the public aware of his new sauce, he would come up with an idea of travelling salesmen touring the country with thousands of miniature bottles of HP Sauce. They would be provided as samples to the public, all carried on small wagons pulled by zebras!

Well, zebras were attractive and would make an immediate visual impact on any high street or village green, Samson thought. But once it was pointed out to him that zebras were virtually impossible to train and hardly the ideal form of transport on the cobbled streets of Great Britain and best left to roam the great expanse of the Serengeti, he refrained from using them. So of the more practical donkeys were agreed upon to pull small promotional carts around the country with free samples of HP Sauce in miniature bottles.

The donkey and carts toured all the main towns of Scotland and England. Hoardings were placed in every major town advertising the sauce in a way no one could possibly miss. The immense cost of the campaign soon reaped rewards, and sales of the sauce dramatically increased. Samson was now able to cut back on his original advertising budget. The sauce was so popular, it was literally selling itself.

A few years later there was another marketing campaign. This time the door-to-door salesmen proudly proclaimed on every doorstep that if the housewife could produce a bottle of HP Sauce, then she would in return be rewarded with ten shillings (50p), quite substantial compared to the low basic weekly wage of seven shillings and sixpence (38p). A male HP Sauce worker at that time could expect on average to have a take home pay of fifteen shillings a week (75p), and a large bottle of HP Sauce could be bought for 6d (2 1/2p).

By the time of the launch of HP Sauce, Edward Eastwood had retired from his wagon business in Chesterfield. His retirement was that of a typical Victorian industrialist, with his many philanthropic activities. He followed his nephew's enterprise with much delight and never missed an opportunity to mention the benefits of HP Sauce to those business associates who knew of his venture with his nephew's brewery.

Eastwood's Wagon Works had built wagons for most of the country's coak and coal merchants. They also built wagons for the Midland Vinegar Company, which bore the HP Sauce logo. Samson Moore, ever the opportunist, would delight in pointing out those wagons to his companions during railway journeys along the ever-increasing network of railways that now criss-crossed the United Kingdom.

HP Sauce within a very short time had become an immense success throughout the United Kingdom. It wasn't long before the sauce had reached equal heights in all four corners of the globe, with sales going to Canada, Sweden, Denmark, and France and as far away as Australia and New Zealand. The next few years would see dramatic export sales. The firm of W. G. Patrick and Co. of Toronto was supplied with orders of five thousand crates of six dozen bottles of sauce at a time. Samson Moore could now claim that his sauce had in fact reached the palates of the world.

With HP Sauce at the forefront of the Midland Vinegar Company, Samson's venture had come a long way in thirty years. Samson himself had also matured into a respected businessman, and in 1905 he was installed as a justice of the peace. He was now a man of high public standing.

1910 will be remembered historically as the year King Edward VII died and for "The Lady with the Lamp", Florence Nightingale. Closer to home, on 11 June, 1910, Edwin Samson Moore's uncle, Edward Eastwood, died. Their partnership had been a great success, spanning over thirty-six years together with the Midland Vinegar Company. At the time of Edward Eastwood's death, the capital of the company had increased to £46,000 (£4,357,000) mainly due to the profits being allowed to accumulate. During their partnership, Edward Eastwood had put £7,000 (£663,000) in hard cash into the business and received in dividends £103,000 (£9,755,000). Edwin Samson Moore received £55,000 (£5,210,000).

Samson was by now in the position to offer the executors of Edward Eastwood's will, George Albert Eastwood (his son) and George Booth, J.P., the sale of his uncle's shares in the company. They were happy to do so and accepted £38,000 (£3,560,000) for his share in the business.

Edwin Samson Moore then became sole proprietor of the Midland Vinegar Company. On 31 December, 1911, he formed a private limited company. It was registered as The Midland Vinegar Company Limited with himself as chairman, Edwin Eastwood Moore as managing director, and Edgar Moore as sales director.

The company was formed with a capital of £100,000 (£9,800,000); £80,000 (£7,800,000) was paid up, with the shares allotted to himself and family. Samson Moore retained sufficient shares to give himself the controlling interest of the business. At a later time, two of the staff were allowed to take approximately £1,000 (£97,000) worth of shares each to qualify themselves as acting directors.

Edward Eastwood had been the silent partner within his nephew's enterprise. He provided the finance to establish the Midland Vinegar Company in 1874, lending his moral support and his own business experience. Samson rewarded the Eastwoods' faith in him. The success of HP Sauce is without doubt Samson Moore's, but one shouldn't forget that without Edward Eastwood's finance, confidence, and trust in his nephew's aspirations, the eventual outcome of Frederick Gibson Garton's HP Sauce would be uncertain.

Edward Eastwood was buried in the Spital Cemetery, Hady Hill, Chesterfield, in the family vault. His epitaph reads: "In Loving Memory of Abigail The Wife of EDWARD EASTWOOD who entered into rest October 11th 1903 aged 76 years. Also of EDWARD EASTWOOD of Tapton who died June 8th 1910 aged 84 years. Founder of Eventide Homes and Donor of medical wards to the Chesterfield Royal Hospital."

MIDLAND VINEGAR Co.

VINEGAR BREWERY.
GOLD MEDALS AWARDED FOR PURITY & EXCELLENCE.

CONTRACTORS TO THE ADMIRALTY

**ASTON CROSS,
BIRMINGHAM.**

SOLE PROPRIETORS OF GARTON'S H.P. SAUCE

Oct.13th.1908

Messrs. Mather & Crowther,
   New Bridge St.,
      London.

Dear Sirs,

    We have much pleasure in expressing our approval of the way in which our instructions for advertising have been carried out, by your service, in which we have every confidence.

                 Yours truly,
        THE MIDLAND VINEGAR Co.

                Edwin G. Moore
                    MANAGING PARTNER

FROM THE MEMORANDUM

MIDLAND VINEGAR CO.

TELEGRAPHIC ADDRESS:
MIDLAND, BIRMINGHAM.
TELEPHONE Nº EAST 193

CONTRACTORS
TO THE
ADMIRALTY.

SOLE PROPRIETORS
OF
H.P. SAUCE.

MALT VINEGAR BREWERS,
ASTON CROSS.
BIRMINGHAM.

Dear Sir, November 25th, 1910.

H.P. Sauce wrappers.

    We are holding a Hand-writing Competition for school children, and all competitors are required to send in a wrapper off a H.P. Sauce bottle, with their writing.

    Will you please give instructions that wrappers shall only be given to purchasers of a bottle of H.P. Sauce.

    In case you have all your stock unwrapped for show purposes, if you give the intending competitors one of your bill-heads, stating that they have bought a bottle of H.P. Sauce, this will be accepted in the competition in lieu of the wrapper.

    The wrapper referred to is the plain transparent paper, in which each bottle is wrapped when it leaves here, and of course has no printed matter on. (Labels or capsules cannot be accepted).

    Copy forms for the Competition will be distributed in your district, and if you would also like a few to distribute among your customers, we should be pleased to forward you a supply on receipt of a request, per enclosed Post Card (which requires no stamp).

    The competition should still further increase the sales of H.P. Sauce, and if this line is prominently displayed, you will derive the full benefit of the money we are spending.

    If you would like any further particulars, we hope you will write us.

        Yours truly,

                Edwin S. Moore

(13)

The Midland Vinegar Company Limited

The second decade of the twentieth century would see great expansion at the "Sauce". When Edward Eastwood and Edwin Samson Moore bought the rights to HP Sauce from Mr Frederick Gibson Garton in that historic agreement of 1899, they also acquired several other sauces, one of which was Daddies Sauce.

Samson Moore had by now proven with the success of HP Sauce that new condiments were acceptable to the public as long as the price remained affordable. HP Sauce was made with quality malt vinegar. Daddies Sauce used less malt vinegar and more of the less-expensive spirit vinegar. This allowed for a brown sauce with a slightly different taste but at a cheaper price. Samson Moore decided to register another company at Aston Cross, The Trade Malt Vinegar Company, which would be used as the trading company for Daddies Sauce so as to distinguish it from and prevent it from possibly damaging the image of HP Sauce. Samson need not have worried. The public were equally appreciative of its low price and its taste, and Daddies Sauce, introduced in 1912, became a firm favourite with the public. It was registered as "Daddies Favourite Sauce" in 1916.

Daddies Sauce was sold in Ireland in 1912, a year that would see further improvements with the company transport. The first Thorneycroft lorry was purchased for deliveries at the brewery. HP Sauce crossed the Atlantic and was sold in the United States in 1913. Motorcycles were also introduced that year, to be used by the sales representatives.

The second decade of the twentieth century brought with it many changes throughout the world. In the United Kingdom, social conditions took a dramatic change when Lloyd George and his fellow Liberals instigated radical social policies. The national insurance scheme was brought into existence. It soon fulfilled its pledge to help all, with its pension and sickness benefits. Employers paid 3d a week, employees put in 4d, and the government contributed 2d a week.

Working conditions continued to improve. But alas, for many of the work force at the brewery and elsewhere across the nation, living conditions that mankind had yet to endure were soon to become the norm in war-torn France.

In June 1914 the lives of Europeans would change forever when in Sarajevo, Archduke Franz Ferdinand was assassinated. The war to end wars had begun. 4 September, 1914, was the date many would not easily forget. In the weeks after the war began, it was rumoured that it would be all be over by Christmas. As the list of casualties increased, most newspapers carried columns of the wounded and missing. The war to end wars affected every family nationwide, not least the workers at Samson's brewery, who faithfully enlisted. This created a short-term staffing problem, which was soon resolved. Samson had always said only single women could join his work force; home was the place for a married woman, not the factory. Samson would soon have to concede. Women were marching for the vote and demanding the right to serve, and with his workforce depleted, his needs were greater than his beliefs. The women were encouraged to keep their men's jobs safe for their return.

The years of the war brought major advancements in technology and science. Unfortunately, one new discovery came too late to save the life of Samson's youngest son, Edgar. In 1915, just a year before insulin was discovered, Edgar died of diabetes. It was a sad loss to his family, already shaken by the many deaths of the workforce.

HP Sauce continued to play a vital role during the war years. The government had large contracts with the Midland Vinegar Company to supply the troops with the sauce. Many of the troops were later to say how the sauce had livened up what had become the all-too-familiar diet of bully beef.

1917 brought with it a new change to the label of HP Sauce. Samson, ever ready to keep pace with changing circumstances, introduced the soon-to-be-familiar famous French paragraph, which praised the contents and excellence of the sauce. The reasons for introducing the text was never made clear, but perhaps it was thought that with so many troops in France, it would only be a matter of time before the French themselves came into contact with the delights of the sauce. What better way of advertising it to them than to allow the French to read the qualities of this great British delight in their own language? Whatever the reasons, the French text soon became a part of the HP Sauce story.

The author's translation of the French paragraph is as follows:

"This prime choice sauce possess the highest digestive qualities and is an assortment of fruits and spices from the orient and east. The pure malt vinegar is absolutely delicious and appetising with hot or cold meat, fish, ham, cheese and salads. It tastes nice with soups, mince, and stews. Only Manufacturers."

Peace did not come that first Christmas. It would be another four years before the Armistice was signed on 11 November, 1918. The losses were great, and the emotional wounds would take a generation to heal. With the war now at an end, the survivors returned to their jobs at the brewery. The post-war period would see the Midland Vinegar Company continue to flourish. Sales of vinegar, pickles, and sauces all increased.

After the end of hostilities, Samson Moore was approaching his seventieth year. He began to take a less active part in the business. In 1920 he retired, and Peter

Holmes was appointed managing director. Samson took to retirement in his stride and continued his visits to his favourite retreats in Birmingham's, Arthur Moore's Oyster Bar and the picturesque Hydro at Matlock Derbyshire.

In 1921, Samson and Mary celebrated their golden wedding anniversary. With it came the early signs that the business Samson had conceived some forty years earlier would soon pass out of the Moore family's hands.

Below left: The author's great-great-grandparents, Mary Moore and Edwin Samson Moore, on the occasion of their golden wedding anniversary, 21 November, 1921.

Samson Moore's son Edwin Eastwood Moore (Eddie) had spent more than twenty years at his father's side. He was fully involved with all the new innovations at the brewery and modern facilities and developments, but he had also been aware of the recent depression of 1922, which had deeply affected business, with the price of vinegar dropping by over 50 per cent from the wartime levels. One reason for this was that during the war the brewery had massive orders for both vinegar and HP Sauce for the front-line troops.

Eddie was fully aware of supply and demand determining the greater part of business success.

Samson, whose health reflected his advanced years, realised that with younger members of the family pursuing other careers and not wishing to join the business, perhaps now was a good time to consider selling. He had a good heart-to-heart discussion with his son Eddie. Would Eddie accept the role of managing director and continue at the helm of the new business? But Eddie was resolute in his decision that he had also committed a large part of his life to the brewery and wished to take early retirement.

Cyril Owen, Eddie's brother-in-law, had previously joined the firm. He had been promoted to sales manager in 1922, and Samson and Eddie knew he was totally committed to the brewery business and would be the obvious candidate as a future managing director.

So with Samson's approval, the business passed into other hands. Eddie made substantial provision for his parents and his seven sisters. Christmas 1924 would be a time of Christian celebration and also a time of reflection of what had been achieved by Edward Eastwood's trust and financial commitment to his nephew, Edwin Samson Moore, in those early days of 1874. That trust, together with Samson and his son Edwin's dedication and hard work, had created a condiment worthy of furnishing the kitchen cupboards of the world.

Edwin "Eddie" Eastwood Moore, taken on his retirement, Christmas 1924.

(14)

HP Sauce Limited

The Midland Vinegar Company Limited was sold to the British Shareholders Trust on 31 December, 1924, for the agreed amount of £650,000 (£31,000,000) payable in cash. The British Shareholders Trust were responsible for financing the more important industrial companies of England at that time, and it was in this capacity that they were responsible for organising the re-sale of the old company, the Midland Vinegar Company Limited, to the new company, HP Sauce Limited. As the new owners, the British Shareholders Trust in an agreement dated 22 January, 1925, agreed to sell to the new company HP Sauce Limited for the sum of £730,000 (£37,000,000).

The purchase of the original business by HP Sauce Limited from the British Shareholders Trust would be financed by sale of shares. The original issued capital was 260,000 preference shares of £1 each and 300,000 ordinary shares of £1 each. The directors and staff of the old Midland Vinegar Company agreed to buy 100,000 ordinary shares at £1=50, giving confidence to future shareholders that the new company would be of equal success to the originators.

The shares would prove to be a solid investment. In 1930 and after a bond issue, the £1 ordinary shares were worth over £6 each, a true reflection of the company Edwin Samson Moore had established some fifty years earlier.

Sir Pierce Lacy (1872-1956), from Edgbaston, Birmingham, practised as a stockbroker in Birmingham and became a partner in Cutler & Lacy. He was also the chairman of the Birmingham Stock Exchange. He founded and was Chairman of both the British Trusts Association in 1917 and the British Shareholders Trust in 1921. He was created a Baronet in the 1921 Birthday Honours for his contribution to finance.

Above: Sir Pierce Lacy the Chairman of the British Shareholders Trust, who in 1924 bought the Midland Vinegar Company from the Moores and then floated it as a public company under the name of HP Sauce Limited.

*This Prospectus has been duly filed with the Registrar of Companies.
Application will be made to the Committees of the London and Birmingham Stock Exchanges for special permission to deal in, and in due course for quotation of the Preference Shares.*

The List of Applications will be closed on or before Wednesday, the 4th February, 1925.

H.P. SAUCE LIMITED,

Successors to THE MIDLAND VINEGAR COMPANY, LTD.

SHARE CAPITAL:

AUTHORISED:		ISSUED OR TO BE ISSUED:
300,000	Ordinary Shares of £1 each	300,000
300,000	7 per cent. Cumulative Preference Shares of £1 each (260,000 now offered for Subscription)	260,007
£600,000		£560,007

of which the 300,000 Ordinary Shares and 7 Preference Shares have already been subscribed.

MIDLAND BANK, LIMITED, 5, Threadneedle Street, London, E.C. 2, and all Branches, are authorised as Bankers for and on behalf of the Company to receive at their respective offices and Branches, applications for the above-mentioned

260,000 Seven per cent. Cumulative Preference Shares of £1 each at par,

payable by the following instalments:—

	£	s.	d.	
On Application		2	6	per Share.
„ Allotment		5	0	„ „
„ 2nd March, 1925		12	6	„ „
	£1	0	0	„ „

Payment may be made in full on allotment or on any date thereafter in advance under discount at the rate of 4 per cent. per annum. Failure to pay any instalment when due will render the amount previously paid liable to forfeiture. Interest at the rate of 10 per cent. per annum will be charged on all instalments in arrear.

Applications from customers, employees and holders of the Shares of the Midland Vinegar Company, Limited, will receive special consideration.

The Certificates for the Preference Shares will be ready in exchange for fully paid Allotment Letters on and after the 23rd March, 1925.

The Shareholders of the Midland Vinegar Company, Limited, have agreed with **The British Shareholders Trust, Limited,** by themselves or their nominees to take up 100,000 of the 300,000 Ordinary Shares at the price of 30/- per Share and the balance of 200,000 Shares have been subscribed by **The British Shareholders Trust, Limited,** and others at the same price, viz., 30/- per Share.

SEVEN PER CENT. CUMULATIVE PREFERENCE SHARES.

The total amount of these Shares is limited to 300,000 Shares of £1 each, of which 260,000 Shares are now being offered, the balance of 39,993 Shares being reserved for future developments.

The following notice in the *London Gazette* of 27 January, 1925, describes one of the last administrative tasks Edwin Samson Moore had to do in the transfer of his business.

The MIDLAND VINEGAR COMPANY Limited

At an Extraordinary General Meeting of the Members of the Company, duly convened and held at the registered offices, 253, Tower-road Aston Cross, Birmingham, on the 7th day of January, 1925, the subjoined Resolutions were duly passed; and at a subsequent Extraordinary General Meeting of the Company, also duly convened, and held at the same place on the 23rd day of January, 1925, such Resolutions were duly confirmed as Special Resolutions:-

Resolutions.

1. That the agreement dated the 24th day of December 1924, and made between the Company of the first part, Edwin Samson Moore of the second part, Edwin Eastwood Moore of the third part and the British Shareholders Trust Limited of the fourth part, being an agreement for the sale and purchase of the goodwill, undertaking and certain of the assets of the Company be and the same is hereby ratified, adopted and confirmed.

2. That having regard to the terms of the said agreement of the 24th day of December, 1924, it is desirable to wind up this Company and accordingly that this Company be wound up voluntarily ; and that Charles Frederick Jones Tranter, J. P., of Silverbirch-road, Erdington Birmingham, be appointed the Liquidator for the purpose of such winding-up.

3. That the said Liquidator be herby authorised to carry into effect the sale of the goodwill, undertaking and certain of the assets of the Company in accordance with the terms of the said agreement of the 24th day of December, 1924.

4. That the said Liquidator be and he is hereby authorised to consent to the change of the name of HP Sauce Limited (to which Company the goodwill, undertaking and assets agreed to be sold by the Company have been re-sold by The British Shareholders Trust Limited) to "HP Sauce (Midland Vinegar) Limited," or to such other name containing as a part thereof the words "Midland Vinegar" as the Directors of HP Sauce Limited shall request.

Dated this 23rd day of January, 1925.

EDWIN S. MOORE, *Chairman of Confirmatory Meeting.*

A second notice in the *London Gazette* of that same date relates to the voluntary liquidation of the Midland Vinegar Company Limited.

The Companies Acts, 1909 to 1917.

*In the Matter of the MIDLAND VINEGAR COMPANY Limited
(In Voluntary Liquidation)*

In pursuance of section 188 of the Companies (Consolidation) Act, 1908, a Meeting of the creditors of the above named Company will be held at 6, Bennetts-hill, Birmingham, on Monday, the 9th day of February, 1925 at 11 o'clock in the forenoon, for the purpose provided for in the said section. The liquidation is for the purposes of reconstruction only. All debts due by the Old Company will be paid in full—Dated this 23rd day of January, 1925.

C. F. J. TRANTER, Silverbirch-road, Erdington, Birmingham, Liquidator.

With these two notices, the new company started to trade as a public company.

On 31 December, 1924, HP Sauce Limited was floated by the British Shareholders Trust. The original issued capital was 300,000 ordinary shares of £1 each and 260,000 preference shares of £1. The share price continued to rise steadily and rapidly, and after a bonus issue in 1930, the £1 ordinary shares stood at over £6.

Samson Moore in the centre enjoying a day out with a shooting party with friends and family; his son Edwin Eastwood Moore sat on the left next to his spaniel.

Photo taken from the Town Hall end of New Street: Arthur Moore's Oyster Bar in Needless Alley, Birmingham, at the junction of New Street, where Samson Moore in his later years would enjoy a morning refresher unbeknown to his son Eddie for many years.

Samson Moore enjoyed the tranquil life at his country estate at Moxhull, where the lakes were open to members of staff from the brewery for a day's angling. Samson Moore would only enjoy a few more years of retirement, and on 21 December, 1926, he passed away peacefully at his beloved Smedleys Hydro in Matlock Derbyshire, a place of refuge from the busy working life for a Victorian and Edwardian businessman.

By January 1926, HP Sauce Limited had been trading as a public company for just over a year. Its only connection with Samson Moore was the new managing director, Cyril Owen, who had married Samson's youngest daughter, Dora Josephine. This was a good decision by the company, as it meant that the transition from the Midland Vinegar Company to HP Sauce Limited would have some continuity during the inevitable changes the new directors would make. This would also help the long-serving members of staff adjust to the new management. They only knew the Moores, having worked in this family business where daughters followed mothers and sons followed fathers to work at the sauce for several generations.

The second half of the 1920s would see many social changes, not least the high unemployment level reaching 3 million, the 1926 general strike, and 1928, when women were given the vote. HP Sauce, however, continued as ever in those uncertain times. Expansion and modernisation were never far away. In the bottling department, many advancements were made. Threads on the bottle necks enabled screw caps to be fitted automatically, and new automatic labelling machines worked flat out. Production was vastly increased with filling, capping, and labelling now all being done in a continuous operation.

The end of the decade was marked with the Wall Street crash of 1929. The outlook for the Western world was only mirrored by the previous years of despair and doom. Aviation had come a long way, and Amy Johnson had flown to Australia, but the start of the new decade brought much uncertainly with it.

The 1930s were to be tempestuous years. The Depression had set in, and the uncertainty of possible war loomed round every political corner. The decade would see many changes in Europe, with the beginning of the German Reich. Adolf Hitler became chancellor of Germany in 1933, and within twelve months he had taken on the role of dictator. At first he wasn't taken seriously, and his only apparent talent was his ability to instil hysteria amongst his followers. It would be a further six years before the full force of his actions would be felt across Europe. With the invasion of Poland on 1 September, 1939, and after repeated requests for the withdrawal of Germany's troops from Poland were ignored, Neville Chamberlain, the prime minister of the day, announced by radio on 3 September to the nation and world at large that "as from 11 a.m. this morning we are now at war with Germany".

On the home front, the 1930s had seen our royal family in conflict with Parliament about divorce and the monarchy.

Edward VIII had become king, but this would be short-lived, and he abdicated after being on his throne for only 325 days. He gave up his right to the throne so he could marry the American lady "Mrs Simpson". The monarchy was soon stabilised with the coronation of King George VI and his Queen Elizabeth.

Meanwhile, back at the "sauce", there were new introductions to the dynamic duo of the HP and Daddies Sauce stable. HP Tomato Ketchup, HP Salad Cream, and HP Mayonnaise were all launched upon the eager public. A more dramatic event occurred in the company's history during 1930, when HP Sauce acquired Lea & Perrins of Worcester. Ever since Samson Moore first launched HP Sauce, he had been aware of the more upmarket sauce of Messrs Lea & Perrins, which since its conception in 1842 had always had its appeal with the aspiring middle and upper classes of Victorian Britain. The merger between the companies after an exchange of shares meant the two brands would please the palates of all the nation's appetites.

However, with the onset of another world war in 1939 and with general shortages incurred, cutbacks were necessary in every department, not least the labelling department. With the need for economy, labels changed. The new economy labels bore the Ministry of Foods insignia. The now famous name of "Garton's" disappeared from the label forever. September 1930 would also see the death of Edwin Samson Moore's wife, Mary. Her demise would bring to an end this Victorian generation.

H.P. Sauce Ltd.

PROPRIETORS OF
MIDLAND VINEGAR CO LTD
AND F. G. GARTON & CO LTD

MALT
VINEGAR
BREWERS

MANUFACTURERS OF:
H.P. SAUCE
DADDIE'S SAUCE
GARTON'S TOMATO KETCHUP
H.P. PICKLE, Etc.

ASTON CROSS
BIRMINGHAM

20th. March 1930.

Dear Sir or Madam,

I am instructed to inform you that an Agreement has been entered into defining the terms for amalgamation, as from 1st. January 1930, of the businesses of H.P. Sauce Limited, and of Lea & Perrins, the old established and well known manufacturers of the original Worcestershire Sauce.

The firm of Lea & Perrins is being converted into a Private Limited Company of the same name, whose shares will be acquired by H.P. Sauce Limited by issue of fully paid Ordinary Shares in the latter Company in satisfaction of the consideration to be calculated in accordance with the terms of the Agreement for amalgamation. In due course, Mr. C.W. Dyson Perrins, Captain J. Allan Dyson Perrins, Mr. Charles F. Dyson Perrins and Mr. Harold Seddon, partners in the firm of Lea & Perrins, will join the Board of your Company and will continue to give their personal attention to the business of Lea & Perrins as before.

The completion of the legal and other work arising under the terms of the Agreement, will take some time, and in due course the necessary Meeting of Shareholders of your Company will be called for the purpose of sanctioning the required increase of Capital, probably about the end of April.

My Board desire me to say that they are of opinion that the merger of interests which will be effected will add further to the reputation and strength of your Company.

Yours faithfully,
T.S. RADFORD,
Secretary.

HP Sauce once again played a significant part during the Second World War. Troops were once again glad to see the sauce included in their rations to liven up their monotonous diet. Women once again took over their male counterparts' jobs, and although staffing levels were low, progress and production continued with everyone doing their bit towards the war effort.

1940 brought with it food rationing. The population were told to "dig for victory", and allotments became the order of the day. Every available plot of land was used in one way or another to produce vegetables. Only varieties limited the eager public's desire to "dig for victory". A typical example of food rations allowed for one person, which had to last a full week, are as follows: bacon and ham 4-oz., butter—2 oz., dried eggs—1 pkt., cheese—2 oz., liquid milk—2 1/2 pints. It would not be until 1954 that food rationing ended.

During the war years, the export of HP Sauce was seriously affected due to heavy losses of merchant shipping. Exports to Canada were impossible. It was decided after some intense and careful deliberation that the only way to meet demand in Canada would be to arrange for HP Sauce to be manufactured there.

Ever since 1899 and Samson Moore's purchase from the Nottingham grocer Frederick Gibson Garton, the recipe of HP Sauce had remained a closely guarded secret. So it was with some trepidation that it was decided to allow E. D. Smith and sons to manufacturer the sauce in Canada. To protect against any possible chance of the recipe falling into competitive hands, the recipe was written in two coded letters, and the equipment and methods of production were sent separately in a third letter. Thus ensured that Canada was able to keep demand satisfied, whilst in the United Kingdom the rationing had put paid to the amount of sauce one could use.

Early in May 1945 the Germans surrendered. On 8 May the country rejoiced, and church bells across the nation rang out to welcome VE Day, victory in Europe. With the end of the war, the country looked forward to a new and better life. But the world's economy was in ruins. Every business had to look after its own interests and make do. Times were hard. They were not made any easier by the worst winter on record in 1946, which carried on into 1947. The railways were paralysed, and roads were blocked with snowdrifts up to ten feet high. Water supplies were erratic, with pipes frozen. Electric and gas supplies were frequently shut off, and bread was rationed again. HP Sauce, like other factories and domestic homes alike, had to "batten down the hatches" as they had during the war and soldier on doing the best they could.

It was not, however, all doom and gloom in those post-war years. In 1947 the future queen, Elizabeth, married Prince Phillip, an occasion that brought warm relief to many. Although central London did its best to brighten up the occasion with bunting and flags festooned over buildings, it was impossible to hide the scars of bombed-out buildings that were still prevalent along the skyline of London. But with the world's media and heads of state assembled, the British did what only the British can do best: to put on a ceremony that would have the approval of the nation, even in those austere times.

HP Sauce had not lost its appeal during those difficult times. The demand for the sauce continued as ever, and the firm was soon back in full production. To meet these increased demands, it was found necessary to acquire a bottle factory. Having already held shares in a company called the Albion Bottle Company of Oldbury, and having established controlling interest in the business, it became a matter of some sense for the Albion Bottle Company to now join the HP Sauce group. Expansion was hindered, however. During the post-war years, building permits remained restrictive, and all plans for new buildings had to wait. To escape these problems, HP Sauce acquired two further family-run businesses, Macks of Walsall and Fletchers, a famous Yorkshire sauce manufacturer. They also joined the now much-enlarged HP Sauce group.

With these new additions, HP Sauce could look forward to continued success and prosperity. The end of the decade saw cars appearing at the brewery and the demise of the last of the dray horses. They had served the firm well and had been a constant reminder of the industrious past history of the company but were now able to spend their retirement in greener pastures. The economy labels also disappeared, although the "French paragraph" would remain for many years to come.

The 1950s would see the premature death of King George VI, who died in 1952. The sadness would soon be replaced with the coronation in June 1953 of Queen Elizabeth. Television, although invented before the war, became more a part of the modern age after the coronation was shown live to a larger audience. At the Sauce, the buildings were festooned with flags and buntings. Street parties and fun for all were the order of the day. The whole nation celebrated together as they had on VE Day a decade earlier. As a sign of the continued blessing of peace and the new era of endeavour, it was the great achievement of Sir Edmond Hilary and his team of Sherpas to on the day of the coronation climb to the peak of the previously unconquered Mount Everest.

The last memorial of the war years disappeared in 1954 with the end of rationing. It was also a time of new excellence in man's quest for human endurance: Dr Roger Bannister became the first man to record a four-minute mile.

The decade had indeed set off at a roaring pace. At HP Sauce, progress had not been deficient in modernisation or new products. Already in 1953, tomato sauce had been launched under the trade name "Daddies Tomato Sauce" to twin with the equally successful brown sauce of "Daddies Favourite". With new products and more variety in food available, it was decided to launch "HP Baked Beans". Beans had long been a part of the American diet, if only captured by the romanticism of cowboy films. The British public were eager to enjoy the delights of their American cousins, and the time seemed right to oblige them. Like all the new HP products, HP Baked Beans were an instant success.

It seemed that progress would once again be affected by world affairs when in 1956 the Suez Canal crisis looked likely to cause great confrontation. The French and British invasion to restore some order in the region only added to fears of the possible loss of supply routes for the much-needed spices and raw materials. After some early worries, the problem did not escalate. As usual at HP Sauce, normality was the order of the day.

The 28 December 1956 was a day many at the brewery would not easily forget. The inhabitants of the surrounding streets also found the following incidents remaining with them for many years. The transport manager, having closed up the offices, was getting ready to leave for home as normal when the foreman rang him from the Top Yard. With despair in his voice he told of a flood, not caused by any heavy rain or water main burst but a flood of vinegar cascading down Tower Road. The manager, at first only half believing what the foreman had said, rushed out to find 45,000 gallons of malt vinegar rushing towards Aston Cross. Three hours of continuous pumping by the fire brigade did not stop the surge of vinegar reaching Aston Road, over a quarter a mile away. Houses were flooded out. Furniture and carpets and all manner of household contents were drenched with the pungency of malt vinegar. However, it wasn't long before Tower Road was back to normal. Efficient compensation from HP Sauce soon helped replace the contents, and the inhabitants soon had their homes spick and span once more.

It wasn't immediately apparent to as the cause of the explosion, and there were few clues amongst the pile of wrecked timbers. The vats were inspected annually. At the last inspection, no faults had been found. One vat, which had been erected in 1906 and stood some fifteen feet above the ground, had during the First World War been strengthened by having a copper plate fixed inside the vat to give the springing staves more support. It is thought that rot must have set in behind the plate, or perhaps the flat steel hoops had rusted out, putting more strain on the others and causing the whole vat to collapse. Whatever the cause, another remarkable chapter had occurred within the story of HP Sauce.

With an extension built in 1957, the appearance of the brewery changed once more. A new building was erected for much-needed storage and despatch departments.

Sporting connections with HP sauce were cemented in 1957, when Aston Villa won the FA Cup. The captain of Villa had a brother in the sales staff at the Sauce, and the cup run had been closely watched by all the employees. They eagerly hoped that their team could get to Wembley and provide the area with a much-needed lift and day out to London. Aston Villa had long been associated with HP Sauce, for the club had established itself nearby to the brewery just as it was founded back in 1874. The club's colours of claret and blue are also used on the bottle labels of HP Sauce.

The 1950s saw many much-needed improvements in living standards and social conditions throughout the country. The memorable words of the prime minister of the day, Harold Macmillan (Super Mac!), "You've never had it so good", still echo in the ears of many families who had lived through the war years and at last could see some hope and future for themselves and their fellow citizens around the world.

Such was the wide appeal of HP Sauce that the poet laureate of the day, John Betjeman, wrote in his *Collected Poems* (1958)

"I pledge her in non-alcoholic wine

And give the HP Sauce another shake".

The Midland Vinegar Brewery HP Sauce

On the right is the chimney stack of the Vulcan Brewery, built in 1886 and carefully banded with metal to preserve the brickwork. The rooms in front were used as bottling shops. The machinery for the first automatic filling lines were hauled by block and tackle through a window. In the centre, the 1957 building; the building on the left was completed in 1967. The poplar tree on the left marks the place where the terraced houses of Park Lane once stood.

The 1960s brought a new era of freedom and fashion, with popular music at the forefront of the new world of the "teenager". The most notable personalities of the decade were four young men from Liverpool. The Beatles, with their collar-length hair and debonair clothes, gave the youth of the country the voice for free expression and individuality.

The farthing, worth one quarter of an old penny, was no longer legal tender, but the monetary headline of the decade was the Great Train Robbery of 1963. The days of just one television channel, BBC One, had long gone, and commercial television had proved a great success. Huge audiences were captivated by the three-minute adverts, which provided as much enjoyment as the programmes in between. HP Sauce, like so many other big businesses of the day, used this modern marketing tool to advertise their own products. The management at the Sauce had not been slow in realising the potential of the small screen. When Midland Television established themselves at the Old Theatre Royal, Aston Cross, HP Sauce took full advantage of the television company's up-to-date advertising and promotion executive teams. With careful and thoughtful planning, the company's products would soon be presented into every living room throughout the country.

Samson Moore would have been enthralled with the technology available to promote these products. There was no need for donkeys and carts travelling through every town and city to advertise them now. Samson was a vivid proponent of the use of mass publicity to catch the public's eye, and the use of this new media would have been met with his full approval.

Harold Wilson, the notorious pipe-smoking politician of the day, became prime minister when the Labour Government came into power in the 1964 general election. Wilson's "white heat of technology" speech was made as a direct result of the loss of manufacturing jobs and the need to be kept at the forefront of new industry and technological advances—the very things that had transformed the country a hundred years before. At the Sauce they knew very well about technological advances; their many departments had over the years continued to modernise and improve wherever possible.

The changing political scene around the world had a major effect on HP Sauce when in 1965 Rhodesia, now Zimbabwe, under the leadership of Ian Smith, declared its independence from Britain. Sanctions left Rhodesia without its much-sought-after sauce.

A far greater tragedy of that year was the death of Sir Winston Churchill, born in the same year, 1874, as the Midland Vinegar Company was established. The whole country stood in quiet respect and bereavement as his coffin was carried down Whitehall, mounted on a solemn gun carriage. The laying to rest of this beloved and respected world figure had only been upstaged by the tragic events of two years earlier, when in 1963 President John Fitzgerald Kennedy was assassinated on Friday, 22 November, a day the free-thinking people of the world stood together in disbelief and outrage and commentators struggled with incoherent words to describe the blood-stained end of another era in American and world history.

It was not all doom and gloom in the second half of the 1960s. At HP Sauce, dramatic changes were on their way. In 1967 the HP Sauce board recommended to its shareholders an offer from Imperial Tobacco Company of 25/—per share, (£1.25) With the shareholders' acceptance, HP Sauce found itself as a subsidiary of the Imperial Tobacco Company. With the new union of management and sales force at the forefront of the company, HP Sauce continued its progress. With Golden Wonder Crisps and Smedleys, the Imperial Group now enlarged its food operation. Ross Foods were later also to join the group, and a new company was re-formed under the name "Imperial Foods Limited".

The new headquarters of the company were at Leamington-Spa. With factories operating all over the United Kingdom, Aston Cross still remained the home of the world's most famous brown sauce and other well-known pickles and sweet sauces.

HP Sauce always kept up to date with the latest fashions and fads of the times. The late 1960s were no exception. With the introduction of takeaway food shops, which seemingly opened up on every street corner, the public's attitude to foreign foods and especially oriental recipes changed. It had become as normal to go out for an Indian or Chinese meal as to the local cinema to see the latest Bond movie. With all these new changes in the British appetite, a new sauce with the flavour and appeal to liven up any oriental dish was launched. HP Fruity Sauce was an immediate success, and once again HP Sauce Limited had been at the forefront of modern demands. With the new products satisfying the public's every whim, the decade came to a close. HP Sauce Limited began to look forward to the inevitable celebrations that would soon transpire as they entered the next decade, which would claim the company's centenary.

Ever since those early days in 1890, when Frederick Gibson Garton claimed his sauce had been seen in the restaurants of the Houses of Parliament, much has been made of the statement that politicians and their guests enjoyed the pungent sauce on their meals. To celebrate the centenary of the Midland Vinegar Company in 1975, a banquet was arranged with over two hundred guests, many distinguished. Amongst them was the prime minister of the day, Harold Wilson. He had been a much-publicised devotee of HP Sauce: his wife, Mary, had once said, "he does have a habit of covering everything cooked with HP Sauce". The remark, however, was to be refuted when the prime minister made his after-dinner speech to congratulate and endorse the success of one hundred years of sauce production at the Tower Road brewery. He made his confession to the astounded assembly that it was not HP Sauce that he in fact poured all over his food and enjoyed but the more upmarket "Lea and Perrins" Worcestershire Sauce. Whether HP Sauce had been used by the prime minister or not, one couldn't help but wonder whether the sauce which had been apparently seen in the Houses of Parliament restaurants one hundred years previously could also be found in the larder of the most famous house in the land, No. 10 Downing Street.

HP Sauce My Ancestors' Legacy

Sir Harold Wilson with his personal bottle of HP Sauce during the centenary celebrations of the Midland Vinegar Company. He also has copy of The Road from Aston Cross, a publication to celebrate the history of Edward Eastwood and Edwin Samson Moore's Midland Vinegar Company and their subsequent custodians, HP Sauce Limited.

The early 1970s marked the era of industrial decline in the United Kingdom. There were many reasons for the turn-about of the industries and manufacturing dominance that the United Kingdom had enjoyed for the past century and a half. Decimalisation was blamed. The continuous confrontation between belligerent unions and poor management had made British industry the laughingstock of manufacturing throughout the world. Pay demands without productivity and strikes for the most trivial reasons, such as insufficient tea breaks, were the order of the day. The miners' strike of February 1972 would be a guide to the future conduct of British Industrial relations. It signalled the apparent suicide of the industrial base built up by the likes of Edward Eastwood, Edwin Samson Moore, Charles Britton, and all those other Victorian fathers of manufacturing who with their hard work created the tens of thousands of jobs which would see generations of the same families in continuous employment. These enterprises would all to—soon disappear, leaving mass unemployment from which the manufacturing base of the country would never recover.

With widespread power cuts, the public began to get a foretaste of things to come. Oil had long been the commodity which affected world prices and trade. In October 1973, the Arab-Israeli war caused oil prices to soar, and the cost of raw materials increased rapidly. There followed the now-infamous three-day week, where factory operations were curtailed to conserve energy for the national grid.

Food manufacturers and their suppliers were exempted from these restrictions, but they were by no means unaffected by the pursuing industrial scene. The employers and employees at HP Sauce had a long-lived reputation for good working and management relations, and as such everyone carried on as they had during both the world wars and other times of uncertainty. More's the pity that many other industries didn't take the same attitude and thus save the millions who would be made redundant in later years as companies reduced staffing numbers in an attempt to be more competitive.

The entry into Europe in 1973 didn't have the impact the general public had been told and persuaded it would. The following years saw mounting difficulties. In 1974, world shortages of basic food and an increase in demand lead to massive price increases and the new "world enemy": inflation! It was a year of price controls, soaring interest rates, and higher taxes and accordingly saw the demise of the Conservative party under "Ted" Edward Heath.

All these ingredients lead to high unemployment, standing at a million in 1975. People began to think of those days in the 1930s of high inflation and intolerable unemployment levels.

At HP Sauce, as through every crisis, production continued, and the workforce were not disparaged by world events. They looked forward to celebrations. 1975, for all its doom and gloom, as we have previously acknowledged marked the centenary of the founding of the Midland Vinegar Company. The rest of the seventies would see hostile economic factors piling one on top of another. The public began to wonder how and when the country would pull itself out of the dismal situation it had found itself in.

Autumn of 1979 would see the sowing of those seeds that would provide for the country's future prosperity. The Conservative party, under the leadership of Margaret Thatcher, swept to power, and history was made with the first British woman prime minister.

It would be the age of monetarist measures. The target, the public enemy number one, was inflation. In 1980 it reached 21.5 per cent, and unemployment trebled, reaching three million by 1982. The country would have worse to come in June of that year, with the Falklands war looking likely to cause serious disruption to world affairs. After a long succession of defeats and conflicts in our home markets and industries, the country stood proud when the Falklands were retaken. British patriotism returned to this once-battered country.

The price for curbing inflation and stabilising the downward trend of the economy had been a high one, with some experts calculating four million unemployed. The British, however, are a resilient race, and the eighties were to see the Conservative Party returned on two more occasions with Mrs Thatcher at the helm.

At HP Sauce, changes were underfoot in 1984, when after some seventy years the French Paragraph label was removed off the sauce bottle. Outcries were heard up and down the country, with letters to the editor of the *Times* enquiring of the paragraph's demise.

The late 1980s would see the country in many respects back on par with the rest of the western world.

Free enterprise was encouraged, and shareholding had dramatically increased, with many of the well-known, previously nationalised industries denationalised and sold off to eager shareholders.

Another change of ownership for HP Sauce came in 1986 when Imperial Food, the food operation of Imperial Tobacco, was sold to the US/UK corporation Hanson. As usual, production continued at Aston Cross without any fuss, just as it had previously done for the past eighty years, regardless of ownership.

HP Sauce in 1987 had its own "Big Bang" share issue. It was, however, not offering shares in HP Sauce but the chance to indulge in another great British food, sausages, with £1 worth of "Bangers" for three neck label tokens. Once again HP Sauce had seized upon up-to-date trends and used the British public's interest in shares to keep HP Sauce in the public eye.

Prime Minister Margaret Thatcher (1979-1993) meets the staff at the Walsall Lithographic Company who supplied all the stationary, labels, etc. for the HP Sauce brands. The company was established in 1884 and moved to the Midland Road, Walsall site in 1926.

In 1993 a coup-de-grace took place in the Conservative Party. Mrs Thatcher was deposed by John Major, who became the party's leader and subsequently the prime minister.

The Thatcher/Major Conservative Party were to govern the country for more than eighteen years, but in May 1997 the country was looking for a complete change in direction. Tony Blair, under the guise of "New Labour", was elected. After being out of government for nearly two decades, the Labour Party would be looked upon by the public and industry at large for new ideas and prosperity that would take the country into the new millennium.

Another change of ownership came at Aston Cross in 1998, when the French food group Danone acquired HP Sauce from the US/UK Hanson Corporation. Production at Aston Cross carried on as normal, detached from the boardroom dramas and with the hope that the new company might indeed expand production and bring in new products. The dawning of another century at the Sauce beckoned.

(15)

Aston Cross to Elst, Holland

After seven years in ownership, the French company Danone decided to sell HP Foods to Heinz in 2006 for £470 million. HP Sauce was part of the HP Foods group, and as in any acquisition the new company always looks for savings, Heinz were no different. As a successful company of some standing, they were not in the habit of putting sentiment before profits. One presumes the line of thought at Heinz was that the Aston Cross factory was in need of substantial investment to bring it up to their other European manufacturing plants.

On the afternoon of 9 May, 2006, Heinz announced the closure of the Aston production line of HP Sauce with a proposed moved to Elst in the Netherlands. The decision to move production to Holland was made apparently to save the company £25 million over the next ten years. The company claim was that the Aston site was only operating three days a week, although this was refuted by workers and union representatives, who countered that the Heinz plant in Elst was underused itself and that Heinz merely wanted to have full capacity at a site they had previously over invested heavily in. 120 jobs would be lost at the Aston Cross brewery, where generations of the same family had worked since Edwin Samson Moore first began vinegar production in 1874.

Members of Parliament, unions, and the residents of Aston Cross formed committees and made their objections clear to Heinz management, but to no avail. Two local businessmen put forward an offer to buy HP Sauce from Heinz, hoping to complete the purchase and thus save the Aston Cross brewery, but once again Heinz had decided not to allow sentiment to touch their decision. It was a sad day in Aston and for the "City of a Thousand Trades" when the pungent aroma that had made the area so distinctive for over a century would evaporate into the Birmingham night sky, just like so many other famous British marques.

Friday, 16 March, 2007, saw the last bottle of HP Sauce coming off the production line, bringing to an end 108 years of sauce.

The factory was demolished in July 2007, and the six-acre site was completely cleared.

East End Foods bought the site in 2007.

With reluctant acceptance of the factory's fate, the workforce at the sauce carried out their last shifts. At 4:30 p.m. on Friday, 16 March, 2007, the final bottle of HP Sauce came off the production line. With it ended Frederick Gibson Garton, Edward Eastwood, and Edwin Samson Moore's legacy to Birmingham and the world at large. The farewell party was held on 23 February, 2007, at Aston Villa football club.

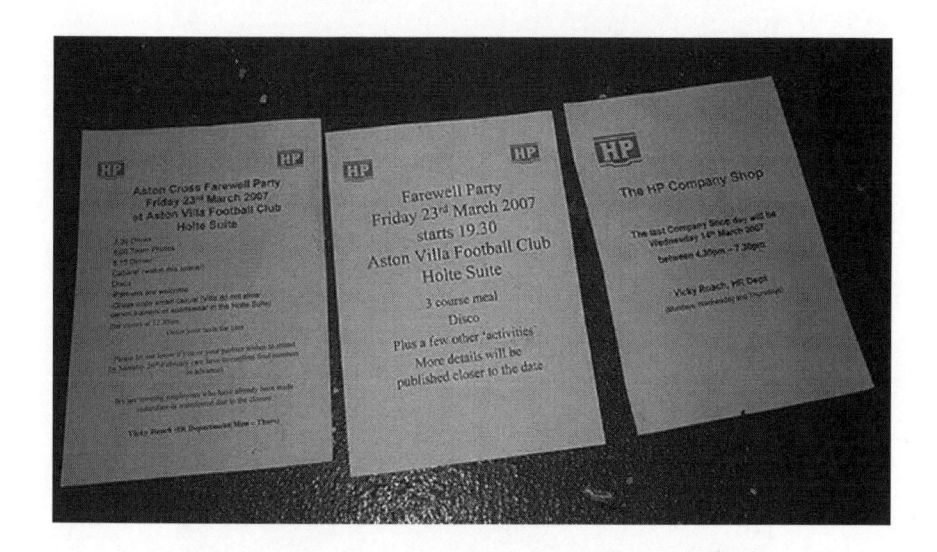

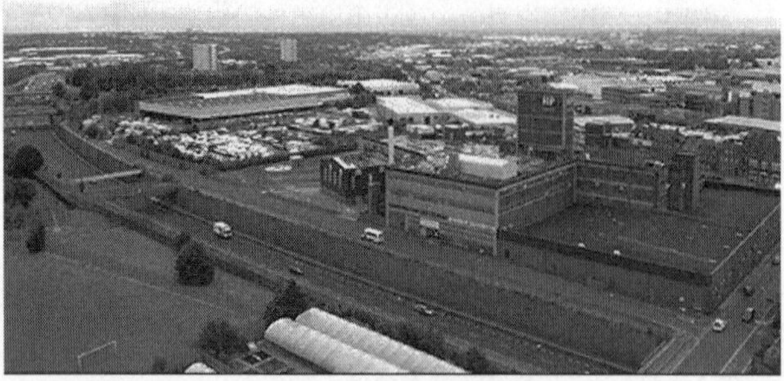

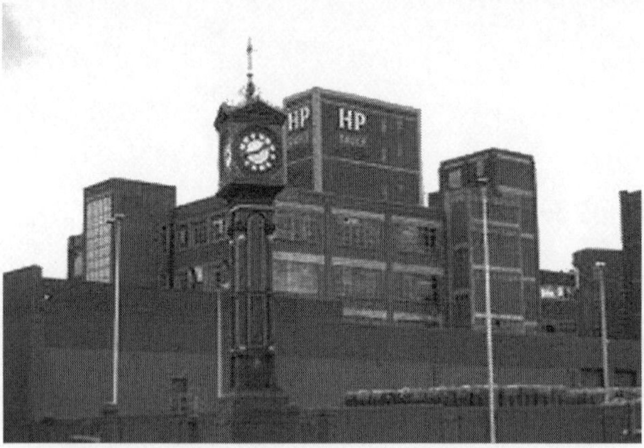
HP
HP

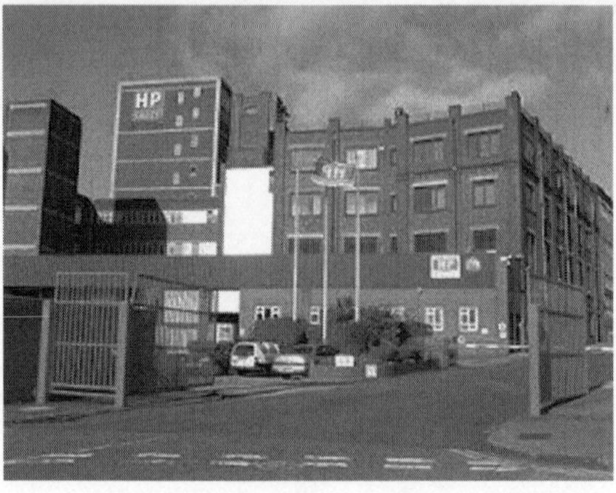
HP
HP

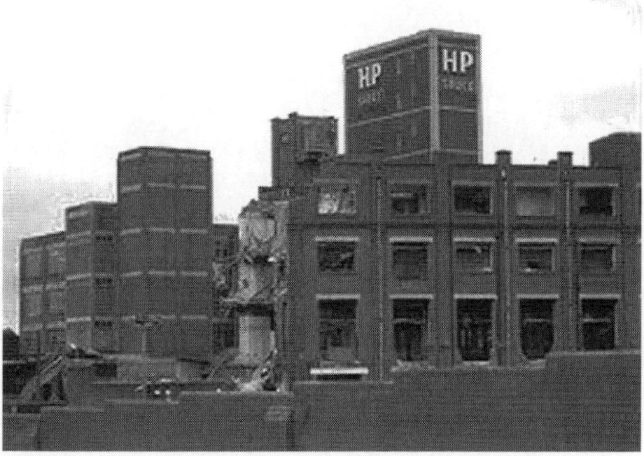
HP
HP

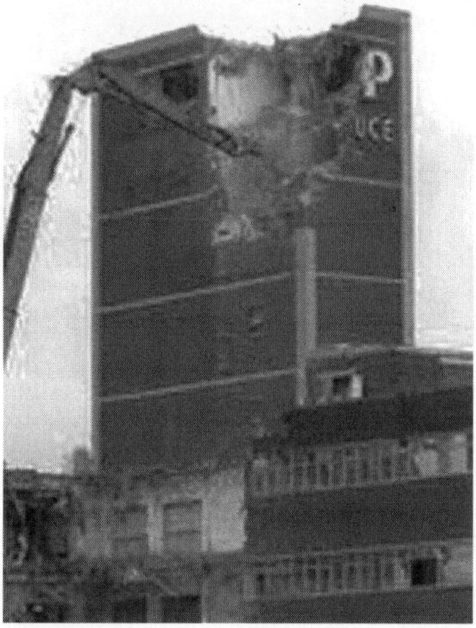

The iconic HP Sauce signs having been removed are now on display in the Birmingham History Galleries, having undergone a thorough restoration by the Galleries conservator.

True, traditional "Brummies" suggested that the iconic signs from the sauce building should be used in some form of artistic "Angel of the North". For decades families using the M6 would use the landmark as a guiding beacon home.

The idea for a commemorative plaque outside the site of the original 1874 Midland Vinegar Company at Aston Cross is being pursued by the author. It would be a fitting tribute to Edward Eastwood, Edwin Samson Moore, and Frederick Gibson Garton.

In the spring of 2013, as the author was putting the final touches to his historical account of this famous British institution and iconic brand, news came that Heinz had accepted an offer from the American billionaire Warren Buffet and his Berkshire Hathaway group, who with the private equity firm 3G had agreed on a purchase price of $28 billion or approximately £18 billion, making it the largest deal in the food industry's history.

At the announcement of the sale on 14 February, 2013, Heinz chairman, president, and chief executive William Johnson said, "The Heinz brand is one of the most respected brands in the global food industry, and this historic transaction provides tremendous value to Heinz shareholders".

Mr Buffett is one of the richest men in the world, having amassed a multi-billion-dollar fortune over decades of investing. His investment expertise has earned him the nickname "the sage of Omaha".

With this latest company acquisition, the history of HP Sauce is passed into another's hand. HP Sauce remains the same as it always has been. The new owners will be fully aware of its history and its previous custodians.

HP Sauce, like Blackpool Tower, the Houses of Parliament, and Sir Winston Churchill can all be best described as icons of the Victorian age. These icons of "Britishness" are recognised throughout the world as symbols of quality, honesty, and good, fair value.

Since its invention in 1894 by the Nottingham grocer Frederick Gibson Garton, HP Sauce has had eight owners, with its present custodian in 2013, some 119 years since its conception, the American industrialist and speculator Warren Buffet.

This former Nottingham cottage industry, this little bottle of brown sauce, this doyen of the condiment world, now sits at the top of the table of one of the world's richest corporations.

From Frederick Gibson Garton via the stewardship of Edwin Samson Moore and his Midland Vinegar Company, HP Sauce has come a long way. Beginning as the settlement for a Victorian grocer's debt to a man far ahead of his time in sales and marketing techniques, HP Sauce was a symbol of continuity throughout the twentieth century. It survived the first Great War, where it was sent to the troops on the front line to give their spirits a much-needed boost and a reminder of home.

The brand remained resolute and steadfast throughout the Depression of the 1930s and the following turbulent years of the Second World War. Changing diets and modern production methods have not daunted the continued success of this, so British an institution.

The additional varieties of sauce, which themselves contributed to the popularity of HP sauce, can be found in abundance on the shelves of supermarkets and food stores across the nation and the world at large.

One thing that can be certain in times of uncertainty, and that is the future of HP Sauce. Maintaining its original format and universal popularity, it will still be around for generations to enjoy well into the twenty-first century and beyond.

As we reach the end of our story, perhaps we can reflect on the legacy our ancestors have given us and raise a glass in celebration. So whether it's served with a traditional British bacon butty, sausage, egg and chips, a good old English fry-up with a nice cup of tea, or perhaps one of the many meat dishes that it also complements, "HP" will always mean that little bottle of brown sauce, that condiment of comfort, that irreplaceable doyen of British cuisine, which can be found in millions of kitchen larders and cupboards across the land. It will forever remain a part of Britain and its great traditions that are known and respected throughout the world today.

(16)

Illustrations and Photographs

Page: Description:
iii Celebrating the 1952 Coronation
v Modern HP Sauce Bottle
ix Britton Pump
ix 1890s Cycle Britain's Soldiers
x Eastwood Wagon HP Sauce Bottle
7 Charles Britton, Leslie Britton, Nigel Britton, Tony Britton, Cherry Britton, Brian Cant, Richard Cant, Fern Britton, Phill Vickery, and Jasper Britton
10 John Boyd Dunlop
12 Richard Lindon Pumps
15 Dunlop Trade Label
19 Britton's Pump Stand
20 Melrose House
22 Sutton Road
22 Holly Lane, Britton Pump
23 Britton Pump
24 William Stanley Britton, Vera Eastwood, and Marion Esther Moore
26 Britton Products Label

27	Brittania Pump
27	Brittania Veloce Pump
27	New Street, Birmingham—Britton Pump
28-29	Britton Wedding
32	Britain's Soldiers
34	Britain's Soldiers
38	William Britain Senior, William Britain Junior, Dennis Britain
42	The Midland Camera Company
43	The Midland Camera Company Catalogue
44	Lee Crescent, Edgbaston, Birmingham
46	The Cambrian Vinegar Company, Leeds
46	Pinks Pickles
49	Winston Churchill
52	Samson Moore and Family, York Lodge
56	Edward Eastwood and Family, Tapton Villa
58	Robert and George Stephenson, Thomas Telford
60	1840s Railway Gang
63	Eastwood Carriage and Wagon Works Interior, Chesterfield
65	Edward Eastwood Wagon
67	Edward Eastwood Oil Painting
68	Eastwood Family, Tapton Villa
69	The Eastwood Brothers
77	George Albert Eastwood
79	Hasland House
83	Eastwood Park Opening Ceremony, 1913
84	George Albert Eastwood Presentation
85	Hasland House 1914, Eastwood Park
86	Hasland House 1988
88	Ringwood Hall

89	C. P. Markham's Fountain
91	Tapton House
98	Eastwood Wagon Plate
98	Eastwood Wagon
98	Midland Vinegar Company Seal
103	1875 Midland Vinegar Company Brewery
106	Mash Tun
106	Midland Vinegar Company Enamel Trade Plate
109	Ansell's & Sons Brewery Heading
109	Drawing: Midland Vinegar Brewery 1875 Floor Layout
111	Moore's Maltine Vinegar Label.
111	Midland Vinegar Company Letterhead
113	Samson Moore's Sales Representatives
116	Conan Doyle—Sherlock Holmes
118	Aston Villa Football Club
124	Harry Palmer
128	Harold Pink
129	Pinks Pickles
131	Houses of Parliament
134	Elizabeth Tower
135	Guy Fawkes
136	*Private Eye*
139	Garton's HP Sauce Bottle
139	Garton's HP Sauce Bottle
140	Garton's HP Sauce Enamel Shop Sign
143	Royal Oak Public House Nottingham
144	Victorian Grocer
145	Frederick Gibson Garton
145	Back-to-back Houses
145	Hand Cart

147	Victorian Copper
148	HP Sauce Recipe
148	Sandon Street, Nottingham
149	HP Sauce Original Bottle
150	Daddies Sauce
151	John Garton
152	Letter from John Garton to Author
159	Victorian Kitchen
166	Victorian Back-street Slum
186	Garton's Custard Essence, Blancmange, HP Sauce
187	Garton's Pickles, Garton's Baking Powder
189	HP Sauce Promotional Donkey and Carts
190	HP Sauce Wagon
192	Edward Eastwood Memorial Stone
193	Midland Vinegar Company Letterhead
198	Daddies Favourite-HP Sauce Bottles
200	World War I Rations and HP Sauce Bottle
201	French Paragraph Label
202	Mary Moore, Samson Moore Wedding Anniversary
204	Edwin Eastwood Moore
208	Sir Pierce Lacy
209	HP Sauce Limited Share Prospectus
211	HP Sauce Share Certificate
212	Samson Moore Shooting Party—Moore's Oyster Bar
213	Moxhull Hall Estate
216	HP Sauce Letter of Proposed Purchase of Lea & Perrins
220	Midland Vinegar Co. 1952 Coronation Celebrations
223	Vulcan Brewery
227	Harold Wilson
230	Margaret Thatcher—Walsall Lithographic

234   Save Our Sauce
235   Farewell Party Invite
236   HP Sauce Factory, Aston Cross, 2006
237   HP Sauce Factory Demolition, 2007
238   Removal of the H & P Sign from the Brewery

(17)

Chronology

1874   Midland Vinegar Company established by Edward Eastwood and Edwin Samson Moore
1875   Malt Vinegar and various pickles produced
1894   **Ownership**: Frederick Gibson Garton invents Garton's HP Sauce
1899   **Ownership Change**: Gartons HP Sauce, Daddies Sauce, and sauce and pickle business acquired as payment for a debt owed to the Midland Vinegar Company
1903   HP Sauce launched nationwide
1904   Daddies Sauce launched
1906   Daddies Favourite sauce introduced
1910   Edward Eastwood dies
1911   Midland Vinegar Company becomes limited corporation after the Eastwood's shares were bought out
1924   **Ownership Change**: Midland Vinegar Company Ltd bought by HP Sauce Ltd
1930   HP Sauce Ltd. Buys out Lea & Perrins shares
1933   HP tomato ketchup, salad cream, and mayonnaise launched

1934	Pikanti introduced
1942	Economy label appears, **Garton** name disappears
1948	Macks, Walsall, and Fletcher's Selby products sold by HP Sauce Ltd.
1952	Distilled malt vinegar introduced
1954	HP Baked Beans and Lea & Perrins Salad Cream introduced
1957	HP tomato soup and Lea & Perrins fruit sauce introduced
1958	New pickles introduced and tomato soup withdrawn
1964	HP Mint Sauce introduced
1967	**Ownership Change**: HP Sauce Ltd acquired by Imperial Tobacco
1968	Pickles sold under Epicure brand name
1969	HP Fruity introduced
1971	Various dessert sauces introduced
1972	A full range of Smedley's canned foods sold by Smedley-HP Foods Ltd
1972	HP Sauce Ltd Amalgamates with Imperial Foods Ltd
1973	Concentrated curry sauce, HP sweet pickle, and Smedley Fruit Pies introduced
1975	HP Sauce celebrates 100 years of the Midland Vinegar Company
1984	Letters to the *Times* about French text removed from label
1986	**Ownership Change**: US/UK corporation Hanson acquires Imperial Foods
1989	HP BBQ Sauce created
1998	**Ownership Change**: French food group Danone acquires Hanson
2005	**Ownership Change**: H.J. Heinz acquires HP Foods Ltd from Danone

2006	Heinz announce the future closure of the Aston production line of HP Sauce
2007	Last bottle of HP Sauce comes off the production line
2007	HP Sauce transfers production to Elst, Netherlands
2007	HP Sauce Tower Road Aston Cross Birmingham Factory demolished
2008	HP Steak Sauce created
2011	HP Guinness Sauce introduced
2012	HP Sauce Facebook page has 100,000 UK fans
2013	**Ownership Change**: Warren Buffett Berkshire Hathaway and private equity firm 3G purchase H.J. Heinz

Acknowledgements

History of advertising trust Norfolk.

Bachmann-Europe

Beamish Museum Northumberland

Eric Evans (Wood and Brass)

H. J. Heinz Company Limited

John Frederick Garton

Chesterfield Library

Geoff Marsden

Birmingham Library

Sir Charles Markham Bt.

Sutton Coldfield Library

AuthorHouse Publishing

Britton-Moore-Eastwood families

Oliver-Hooton-Green families

The many generations of hard-working "Brummies" of Aston Cross

Best Quality only
MIDLAND
VINEGAR
VINEGAR BREWERY
MIDLAND VINEGAR COMPANY

GARTON'S
H.P.
SAUCE
HOUSES OF PARLIAMENT
IS A COMBINATION OF THE CHOICEST
ORIENTAL FRUITS
SPICES AND
PURE MALT VINEGAR
DIGESTIVE RELISH
GARTONS

HP
HP
SAUCE

DADDIES
SAUCE
HP
SAUCE

HP
SAUCE
PROPER
BRITISH

MIDLAND VINEGAR COMPANY

Printed in Great Britain
by Amazon.co.uk, Ltd.,
Marston Gate.